C

Auxiliary Sciences of History

Library of Congress Classification
2008

Prepared by the Cataloging Policy and Support Office
Library Services

LIBRARY OF CONGRESS
Cataloging Distribution Service
Washington, D.C.

This edition cumulates all additions and changes to class C through Weekly List 2008/15, dated April 9, 2008. Additions and changes made subsequent to that date are published in weekly lists posted on the World Wide Web at

<http://www.loc.gov/aba/cataloging/classification/weeklylists/>

and are also available in *Classification Web*, the online Web-based edition of the Library of Congress Classification.

Library of Congress Cataloging-in-Publication Data

Library of Congress.
   Library of Congress classification. C. Auxiliary sciences of history / prepared by the Cataloging Policy and Support Office Library Services. — 2008 ed.
      p. cm.
   "This edition cumulates all additions and changes to class C through Weekly List 2008/15, dated April 9, 2008. Additions and changes made subsequent to that date are published in weekly lists posted on the World Wide Web ... and are also available in *Classification Web*, the online Web-based edition of the Library of Congress classification."
   Includes index.
   ISBN-13: 978-0-8444-1209-2
   ISBN-10: 0-8444-1209-0
   1. Classification, Library of Congress. 2. Classification—Books—Auxiliary sciences of history. I. Library of Congress. Cataloging Policy and support Office. II. Title. III. Title: Auxiliary sciences of history.
   Z696.U5C 2008   025.4'69—dc22   2008015970

For sale by the Library of Congress Cataloging Distribution Service, 101 Independence Avenue, S.E., Washington, DC 20541-4912. Product catalog available on the Web at **www.loc.gov/cds**.

PREFACE

The first edition of Class C, *Auxiliary Sciences of History*, was published in 1915, the second in 1947, the third in 1974, and the fourth in 1993. A 1996 edition cumulated additions and changes that were made during the period 1993-1996. This 2008 edition cumulates additions and changes made since the publication of the 1996 edition.

In the Library of Congress Classification schedules, classification numbers or spans of numbers that appear in parentheses are formerly valid numbers that are now obsolete. Numbers or spans that appear in angle brackets are optional numbers that have never been used at the Library of Congress but are provided for other libraries that wish to use them. In most cases, a parenthesized or angle-bracketed number is accompanied by a "see" reference directing the user to the actual number that the Library of Congress currently uses, or a note explaining Library of Congress practice.

Access to the online version of the full Library of Congress Classification is available on the World Wide Web by subscription to *Classification Web*. Details about ordering and pricing may be obtained from the Cataloging Distribution Service at:

<http://www.loc.gov/cds/>

New or revised numbers and captions are added to the L.C. Classification schedules as a result of development proposals made by the cataloging staff of the Library of Congress and cooperating institutions. Upon approval of these proposals by the weekly editorial meeting of the Cataloging Policy and Support Office, new classification records are created or existing records are revised in the master classification database. Weekly lists of newly approved or revised classification numbers and captions are posted on the World Wide Web at:

<http://www.loc.gov/aba/cataloging/classification/weeklylists/>

Millicent Wewerka, senior subject cataloging policy specialist in the Cataloging Policy and Support Office, is responsible for coordinating the overall intellectual and editorial content of class C. Kent Griffiths, assistant editor of classification schedules, is responsible for creating new classification records, maintaining the master database, and creating index terms for the captions.

Barbara B. Tillett, Chief
Cataloging Policy and Support Office

April 2008

OUTLINE

	Auxiliary sciences of history (General)
1	Periodicals. Serials
2	Societies
3	Congresses
(4)	Yearbooks
	see C1
	Collected works (nonserial)
5	Several authors
7	Individual authors
8	Dictionaries. Encyclopedias
20	Study and teaching
40	General works
45	General special
50	Addresses, essays, lectures
51.A-Z	By region or country, A-Z

CB

History of civilization
  Class here general works only; for individual countries, see classes
    D-F
  Cf. AZ19.2+ History of scholarship and learning
  Cf. CC1+ Archaeology
  Cf. D16.7+ Philosophy of history
  Cf. GN1+ Anthropology
  Cf. GT1+ Manners and customs
  Cf. HM401+ Sociology

3	Periodicals. Societies. Serials
3.5	Congresses
(4)	Yearbooks
	see CB3
	Collected works (nonserial)
5	Several authors
7	Individual authors
9	Dictionaries. Encyclopedias
13	Pictorial works
	Cf. D12 Pictorial atlases
	Historiography
15	General works
	Biography of historians
17	Collective
18.A-Z	Individual, A-Z
19	Philosophy. Theory
20	Study and teaching
	General works
	Early through 1800
23	Latin
25	American and English
27	French
29	German
31	Italian
33	Spanish
35.A-Z	Other, A-Z
	1801-
	American
51	1801-1849
	1850-1950
53	Comprehensive treatises and advanced textbooks
57	Elementary textbooks. Juvenile works
58	Outlines, syllabi, etc.
59	1951-1973
	English
61	1801-1849
	1850-1950
63	Comprehensive treatises and advanced textbooks

CB

General works
  1801-
    English
      1850-1950 -- Continued

67	Elementary textbooks. Juvenile works
68	1951-1973

     American and English, 1974-

69	Comprehensive treatises and advanced textbooks
69.2	Elementary textbooks. Juvenile works

    French

71	1801-1849
	1850-1950
73	Comprehensive treatises and advanced textbooks
77	Elementary textbooks. Juvenile works
	1951-
78	Comprehensive treatises and advanced textbooks
78.2	Elementary textbooks. Juvenile works

    German

81	1801-1849
	1850-1950
83	Comprehensive treatises and advanced textbooks
87	Elementary textbooks. Juvenile works
88	1951-

    Italian

91	1801-1849
93	1850-1950
94	1951-

    Spanish

101	1801-1849
103	1850-1950
104	1951-
113.A-Z	Other languages, A-Z

      e.g.

113.D8	Dutch
113.H8	Hungarian
113.L5	Lithuanian
113.P8	Portuguese
113.R8	Russian
113.S3	Scandinavian
113.S4	Serbian
151	General special

    Including special aspects and relations of the history of civilization
Relations to special topics see CB439.2+

156	Terrestrial evidence of interplanetary voyages. Influence of extraterrestrial life on human civilization
	Cf. BF2050+ Human-alien encounters
	Cf. QB54 Extraterrestrial life
	Cf. TL789+ Unidentified flying objects
	Forecasts of future progress
158	Methodology
	Special forecasts. By author or title
160	Published through 1950
161	1951-
	Civilization and race
	For race relations in general, see HT1501+
	For race relations within particular regions or countries, see classes D - F
	Cf. GN281+ Physical anthropology
195	General works
197	General special
	Educational aspects. Intercultural education
	e.g. education to promote intergroup understanding see LC1099
	Special civilizations
	Including civilizations associated with particular races (or other major groups)
	For the civilizations of particular regions or countries, see classes D - F
	Cf. GN537+ Ethnology
	Caucasian. Aryan
201	General works
	Europe
	For works on European civilization limited to particular centuries before 1800, see CB353.7+
203	General works
204	19th century
205	20th century
206	Alpine. Celtic
	Nordic
213	General works
214	General special
216	Anglo-Saxon
	Mediterranean. Latin
224	General works
226	Spanish
231	Slavic
235	Black
	Semitic
241	General works
	Jewish see BM1+; DS112+

	Archaeology
	Class here general works only; for the antiquities of particular regions or countries, see classes D - F; GN803+
	Cf. DE-DG, Classical antiquities
	Cf. CN1+ Inscriptions
	Cf. GN700+ Prehistoric archaeology
	Cf. N5320+ Ancient art
	Cf. T37 Industrial archaeology
	Periodicals. Serials
1.A1-.A5	Polyglot
1.A6-Z	American. English
3	French
5	German
9	Italian
13.A-Z	Other. By language, A-Z
(15)	Yearbooks
	see CC1+
	Societies
20	International
21	American (United States)
22	Dutch
23	English
25	French and Belgian
27	German, Austrian, and Swiss
29	Greek
31	Italian
33	Scandinavian
35	Slavic
37	Spanish and Portuguese
39.A-Z	Other. By language, A-Z
51	Congresses
	Exhibitions. By place
	see subclasses AM, GN, or N
55	Museums and collections
	Cf. GN800+ Prehistoric archaeology
	Collected works (nonserial)
65	Several authors
67	Individual authors
70	Dictionaries. Encyclopedias
	Philosophy. Theory
72	General works
72.4	Social archaeology
72.7	Classification
	Methodology
	General works
73	Through 1800
75	1801-

	Philosophy. Theory
	Methodology
	Special methods borrowed from other disciplines, A-Z --
	Continued
79.G46	Geophysics
79.I44	Imaging systems
79.M33	Magnetometry
79.M47	Metallurgy
79.M55	Mineralogy
79.P4	Petrology
	Photogrammetry see CC79.P46
79.P46	Photography. Photogrammetry
79.P5	Physics
	Psychic research see BF1045.A74
79.R3	Radiography
79.S33	Scanning electron microscopy
79.S6	Soil analysis
79.S65	Spectrum analysis
79.X73	X-ray spectroscopy
79.3	Processing of the excavated remains
	Including examination, storage, etc.
	Cf. AM141+ Museum technique
	Cf. CC135+ Preservation of antiquities
79.5.A-Z	Remains of special materials, A-Z
79.5.A5	Animal
79.5.B37	Basketwork
79.5.B64	Bone implements
79.5.F53	Fibulae (Fasteners) remains
79.5.H85	Human remains
79.5.I94	Ivories
79.5.J48	Jewelry
79.5.M35	Marine mammals
79.5.N6	Nonartifactual
79.5.P5	Plant
79.5.P58	Pollen
79.5.P6	Pottery
79.5.S76	Stone implements
79.5.T48	Textile fabrics
	Analysis and interpretation of archaeological evidence
80	General works
80.4	Data processing
80.6	Quantitative methods. Statistical methods
81	Environmental archaeology
81.5	Experimental archaeology
	Communication of information. Documentation
82	General works
82.3	Drawings

	Communication of information. Documentation -- Continued
82.6	Report writing
82.8	Information services
82.9	Computer network resources
	Including the Internet
	Study and teaching. Research
83	General works
	Audiovisual aids
85	General works
85.Z9	Catalogs
	Slides
90	General works
90.Z9	Catalogs
	By region or country
	Class individual institutions by country without further subdivisions
95	United States
97.A-Z	Other regions or countries, A-Z
	History of the science of archaeology
100	General works
101.A-Z	By region or country, A-Z
107	Archaeology as a profession
	Biography
	For archaeologists specializing in historical periods of particular countries, see the country in classes D - F, e.g. DF212, Ancient Greece
110	Collective
115.A-Z	Individual, A-Z
	Directories
120	General
	By region or country
123	United States
125.A-Z	Other regions or countries, A-Z
(130)	Laws, regulations, etc.
	see class K
	Preservation, restoration, and conservation of antiquities.
	Antiquities and state
	Including historic (and artistic) monuments, landmarks, etc.
	Class here general works only; for the antiquities or monuments of particular regions or countries, see classes DA-F
	For works limited to specific kinds of landmarks, see the subject, e.g. NA9053.C6
	For works limited to fine art see N8849+
	For works limited to architectural monuments see NA105+
135	General works
136	Government encouragement and support
137.A-Z	Special materials, A-Z

Preservation, restoration, and conservation of antiquities.
Antiquities and state
Special materials, A-Z -- Continued

137.C5	Clay tablets
137.M48	Metal
137.T4	Textile fibers
137.W6	Wood
138	Museum technique
140	Forgeries of antiquities
150	Dealers' catalogs

General descriptive works
Including general European antiquities

160	Through 1800
165	1801-
168	Pictorial works
171	Juvenile works
173	Addresses, essays, lectures
175	General special
176	Extinct cities

Miscellaneous subjects
Bells. Campanology
Cf. ML1039 History of carillons and carillon music
Cf. MT710 Carillon instruction
Cf. NK3653 Decorative bells
Cf. TS583+ Bell founding
General works

200	Through 1800
205	1801-
206.A-Z	Biography, A-Z

Including the history of foundries and lists of their products

207	Juvenile works

By region or country
United States

208	General works
209.A-Z	By region or state, A-Z

Great Britain

210	General works
212.A-Z	English counties, A-Z
213.A-Z	English cities towns, etc., A-Z

Northern Ireland

214	General works
215.A-Z	Local, A-Z

Scotland

216	General works
217.A-Z	Local, A-Z

Wales

218	General works

	Miscellaneous subjects
	Bells. Campanology
	By region or country
	Great Britain
	Wales -- Continued
219.A-Z	Local, A-Z
	Ireland
219.4	General works
219.6.A-Z	Local, A-Z
	France
220	General works
221.A-Z	Departments, regions, etc., A-Z
222.A-Z	Cities, towns, etc., A-Z
	Germany
230	General works
231.A-Z	States, A-Z
232.A-Z	Cities, towns, etc., A-Z
	East Germany
	see CC330+
(234)	General works
(236.A-Z)	Local, A-Z
250.A-Z	Other regions or countries, A-Z
	Casting see TS583+
253	Installation. Maintenance
(255)	Change ringing
	For instruction see MT710-MT711
	For history of change ringing see ML1039
260	Cowbells
	Crosses
	Class here outside crosses and calvaries only
	Cf. BV160 Christian symbols and symbolism
	Cf. NK8428 Metal crosses (Decorative arts)
	General works
300	Through 1800
305	1801-
	By region or country
	Great Britain
310	General works
312.A-Z	English counties, A-Z
	e.g.
312.G5	Gloucestershire
312.S3	Salop. Shropshire
312.S5	Somerset
313.A-Z	English cities, towns, etc., A-Z
	Northern Ireland
314	General works
314.5.A-Z	Local, A-Z

	Miscellaneous subjects
	Crosses
	By region or country
	Great Britain -- Continued
	Scotland
315	General works
315.5.A-Z	Local, A-Z
	Wales
316	General works
316.5.A-Z	Local, A-Z
	Ireland
317	General works
318.A-Z	Local, A-Z
	France
320	General works
321.A-Z	Departments, regions, etc., A-Z
322.A-Z	Cities, towns, etc., A-Z
	Germany
330	General works
331.A-Z	States, A-Z
332.A-Z	Cities, towns, etc., A-Z
	East Germany
	see CC330+
(334)	General works
(335.A-Z)	Local, A-Z
350.A-Z	Other regions or countries, A-Z
	Boundary stones
600	General works
605.A-Z	By region or country, A-Z
	Stone heaps, cairns, etc., of unknown purpose
	Cf. GN790 Menhirs, dolmens, etc.
700	General works
705.A-Z	By region or country, A-Z
710	Hill figures
	Tombs see CC77.B8
960	Lanterns of the dead
	For sculpture see NB1800+

Diplomatics. Archives. Seals
 Cf. Z105+ Paleography
 Cf. Z6601+ Manuscripts
 Diplomatics
  Periodicals. Serials. By language of publication

1	Polyglot
4	English
7	French
9	German
11	Italian
12	Russian
13	Spanish
15.A-Z	Other languages, A-Z
	Societies
20	International
	By region or country
22	United States
23	Great Britain
24	France
25	Germany
	Including West Germany
25.5	East Germany
26	Italy
27.A-Z	Other regions or countries, A-Z
	Congresses
28	By date
	Subarrange by name of the congress
29	With permanent organization. By name
	Collected works (nonserial)
31	Several authors
33	Individual authors
	Dictionaries. Encyclopedias
40	General works
45	Abbreviations, etc.
	Cf. Z111 Paleography
	Philosophy. Theory
46	General works
	Relation to seals see CD5035
47	History of diplomatics
	Cf. Z107+ History of paleography
	General works
50	Through 1680
	1681-1820
51	France
53	Germany
55	Italy
59.A-Z	Other regions or countries, A-Z

	Diplomatics
	General works -- Continued
	1821-
	France
61	General works
62	General special
63	Germany
	Including West Germany
64	East Germany
65	Great Britain
67	Italy
69.A-Z	Other regions or countries, A-Z
	Practice of special chancelleries
70	Rome
	France
71	General works
71.3	Merovingian
71.5	Carlovingian
71.8	Reigns. By date of reign
	Subarrange by author
72.A-Z	Local, A-Z
	Subarrange, under each, by date
	Germany
73	General works
73.5	Reigns. By date of reign
	Subarrange by author
74.A-Z	Local, A-Z
	Subarrange, under each, by date
	Italy
	Papal chancellery
75.A2	Collected works
75.A3	Official regulations, etc. By date
75.A5-Z	General works
75.3	General special
76	General works
77.A-Z	Local, A-Z
	Subarrange, under each, by date
79.A-Z	Other regions or countries, A-Z
	Formularies
80	General works
81.A-Z	Special topics, A-Z
81.P7	Prefaces
81.T8	Transcriptions
81.T83	Translations
87	Forgeries of documents
	Collections of documents, facsimiles, etc., for study
	Cf. D-DU, History (Sources and documents)

	Diplomatics
	Collections of documents, facsimiles, etc., for study --
	Continued
91	General works
93	General special
	Including collections on special aspects, miscellaneous
	collections of the middle ages, etc.
95	By century
	e. g. CD95 7th century
	By region or country
	Europe
101	General works
102	Other
	Great Britain
105	General works
106	Other
	England
109	General works
110	General special
111.A-Z	Provinces, A-Z
112.A-Z	Cities, towns, etc., A-Z
	Scotland
113	General works
114	General special
115.A-Z	Provinces, A-Z
116.A-Z	Cities, towns, etc., A-Z
	Wales
116.1	General works
116.2	General special
116.3.A-Z	Provinces, A-Z
116.4.A-Z	Cities, towns, etc., A-Z
	Ireland
117	General works
118	General special
119.A-Z	Provinces, A-Z
120.A-Z	Cities, towns, etc., A-Z
	Austria
121	General works
122	General special
123.A-Z	Provinces, A-Z
124.A-Z	Cities, towns, etc., A-Z
	Czechoslovakia
124.5	General works
124.6	General special
124.7.A-Z	Provinces, A-Z
124.8.A-Z	Cities, towns, etc., A-Z
	Hungary

Diplomatics
 Collections of documents, facsimiles, etc., for study
  By region or country
   Europe
    Hungary -- Continued

125	General works
126	General special
127.A-Z	Provinces, A-Z
128.A-Z	Cities, towns, etc., A-Z

    France

131	General works
132	General special
133.A-Z	Provinces, A-Z
134.A-Z	Cities, towns, etc., A-Z

    Germany
     Including West Germany

135	General works
136	General special
137.A-Z	Provinces, A-Z
138.A-Z	Cities, towns, etc., A-Z

    East Germany

138.5	General works
138.6	General special
138.7.A-Z	Provinces, A-Z
138.8.A-Z	Cities, towns, etc., A-Z

    Greece

139	General works
140	General special
141.A-Z	Provinces, A-Z
142.A-Z	Cities, towns, etc., A-Z

    Italy

143	General works
144	General special
145.A-Z	Provinces, A-Z
146.A-Z	Cities, towns, etc., A-Z

    Netherlands

147	General works
148	Other

    Belgium

151	General works
152	General special
153.A-Z	Provinces, A-Z
154.A-Z	Cities, towns, etc., A-Z

    Luxembourg

159	General works
160	Other

    Russia. Former Soviet republics

Diplomatics

Collections of documents, facsimiles, etc., for study

By region or country

Europe

Russia. Former Soviet republics -- Continued

161	General works
162	General special
163.A-Z	Provinces, A-Z
164.A-Z	Cities, towns, etc., A-Z

Poland

165	General works
166	General special
167.A-Z	Provinces, A-Z
168.A-Z	Cities, towns, etc., A-Z

Scandinavia

169	General works
170	Other

Denmark

171	General works
172	General special
173.A-Z	Provinces, A-Z
174.A-Z	Cities, towns, etc., A-Z

Iceland

175	General works
176	Other

Norway

177	General works
178	General special
179.A-Z	Provinces, A-Z
180.A-Z	Cities, towns, etc., A-Z

Sweden

181	General works
182	General special
183.A-Z	Provinces, A-Z
184.A-Z	Cities, towns, etc., A-Z

Spain

186	General works
187	General special
188.A-Z	Provinces, A-Z
189.A-Z	Cities, towns, etc., A-Z

Portugal

190	General works
191	General special
192.A-Z	Provinces, A-Z
193.A-Z	Cities, towns, etc., A-Z

Switzerland

195	General works

Diplomatics
Collections of documents, facsimiles, etc., for study
By region or country
Europe
Switzerland -- Continued
196 General special
197.A-Z Cantons, A-Z
198.A-Z Cities, towns, etc., A-Z
Balkan States
200 General works
Albania
202 General works
203 Other
Bulgaria
204 General works
205 General special
206.A-Z Provinces, A-Z
207.A-Z Cities, towns, etc., A-Z
Romania
210 General works
211 General special
212.A-Z Provinces, A-Z
213.A-Z Cities, towns, etc., A-Z
Yugoslavia
214 General works
215 Other
Asia
221 General works
Saudi Arabia
223 General works
224 Other
China
225 General works
226 Other
Indonesia
227 General works
228 Other
India
229 General works
230 Other
Burma. Myanmar
231 General works
232 Other
Vietnam
233 General works
234 Other
Thailand

Diplomatics
   Collections of documents, facsimiles, etc., for study
     By region or country
       Asia
         Thailand -- Continued

235	General works
236	Other
	Japan
238	General works
239	General special
240.A-Z	Provinces, A-Z
241.A-Z	Cities, towns, etc., A-Z
	Iran
243	General works
244	Other
	Philippines
245	General works
246	General special
247.A-Z	Provinces, A-Z
248.A-Z	Cities, towns, etc., A-Z
	Siberia. Former Soviet republics in Asia
249	General works
250	Other
	Turkey
251	General works
252	Other
254.A-Z	Other regions or countries, A-Z
	Africa
255	General works
	Egypt
257	General works
258	Other
	Algeria
260.2	General works
260.3	General special
260.4.A-Z	Provinces, A-Z
260.5.A-Z	Cities, towns, etc., A-Z
	Ethiopia
261.2	General works
261.3	General special
261.4.A-Z	Provinces, A-Z
261.5.A-Z	Cities, towns, etc., A-Z
	Kenya
262.2	General works
262.3	General special
262.4.A-Z	Provinces, A-Z
262.5.A-Z	Cities, towns, etc., A-Z

Diplomatics
Collections of documents, facsimiles, etc., for study
By region or country
Africa -- Continued
Morocco
263.2   General works
263.3   General special
263.4.A-Z   Provinces, A-Z
263.5.A-Z   Cities, towns, etc., A-Z
South Africa
264.2   General works
264.3   General special
264.4.A-Z   Provinces, A-Z
264.5.A-Z   Cities, towns, etc., A-Z
Tanzania
265.2   General works
265.3   General special
265.4.A-Z   Provinces, A-Z
265.5.A-Z   Cities, towns, etc., A-Z
Zaire
266.2   General works
266.3   General special
266.4.A-Z   Provinces, A-Z
266.5.A-Z   Cities, towns, etc., A-Z
Zambia
267.2   General works
267.3   General special
267.4.A-Z   Provinces, A-Z
267.5.A-Z   Cities, towns, etc., A-Z
269.A-Z   Other regions or countries, A-Z
Australia
271   General works
272   Other
New Zealand
289   General works
290   Other
291.A-Z   Pacific islands, A-Z
America
301   General works
North America
305   General works
United States
309   General works
311.A-Z   Special regions or states, A-Z
Canada
331   General works
332   Other

	Diplomatics
	Collections of documents, facsimiles, etc., for study
	By region or country
	America
	North America -- Continued
	Mexico
333	General works
334	Other
	Central America
335	General works
	Belize
337	General works
338	Other
	Costa Rica
339	General works
340	Other
	Guatemala
341	General works
342	Other
	Honduras
343	General works
344	Other
	Nicaragua
345	General works
346	Other
	Panama
347	General works
348	Other
	El Salvador
349	General works
350	Other
	West Indies
351	General works
	Bahamas
353	General works
354	Other
	Cuba
355	General works
356	Other
	Haiti
357	General works
358	Other
	Jamaica
359	General works
360	Other
	Puerto Rico
361	General works

CD

Diplomatics
  Collections of documents, facsimiles, etc., for study
    By region or country
     America
      South America
       Venezuela -- Continued

392	Other
	Study and teaching
501	General works
505	General special
511.A-Z	By region or country, A-Z

      Under each country:

	.x	*General works*
	.x2A-.x2Z	*Schools. By city, A-Z*

Archives
  Class here (1) Works on the science, methodology, etc., of
     archives; (2) Guides to depositories; and (3) Inventories,
     checklists, calendars, etc., of public or academic and religious
     institutional records, historic documents and official papers,
     including those of families
  For transcriptions of records, see the subject of the records in
     classes B - Z
  For inventories, checklists, calendars, etc., of other institutional
     records, see bibliography of subject in classes K, M, or Z
  For inventories or lists that combine both public records
     and private papers see CD1000+
  For lists of private papers (including records) of an
     individual see Z6616.A3+

921	Periodicals. Societies. Serials

     For the archives of individual societies, see CD1169, CD1377,
      CD1657, etc.

923	Congresses
	Collected works on the science of archives (nonserial)
931	Several authors
935	Individual authors
941	Directories (General)

     For directories of particular countries see CD101+

945	Dictionaries. Encyclopedias
947	Philosophy. Theory
	General works on the science of archives

    Including general administration of archives

950	American and English
952	Dutch
953	French
955	German
957	Italian
958	Scandinavian

Archives

General works on the science of archives -- Continued

959	Spanish and Portuguese
965.A-Z	Other languages, A-Z
	e.g.
965.R8	Russian
971	General special
972	Addresses, essays, lectures
973.A-Z	Special methods and techniques, A-Z
973.A37	Acquisition
973.A77	Appraisal
	Cataloging see Z695.2
	Conservation, restoration, etc. of books see Z700.9+
	Conservation, restoration, etc. of manuscripts see Z110.C7
973.D3	Data processing
973.D53	Digitization
	Photographic methods see Z265+
	Special categories of archives
	For archives on special topics, see the topic in classes B - Z
	For medical archives see R119.8
973.2	Audiovisual archives
974	Church archives
974.4	Documents in machine-readable form. Electronic records. Databases
	Cf. ZA4081.86 Institutional repositories
976	Family archives
976.5	Municipal archives
977	Personal archives
	Buildings
981	General works
	Equipment. Furniture
983	General works
985.A-Z	Special, A-Z
	By region or country see CD1000+
	Individual archives see CD1000+
986	Security measures
986.5	Access control to public records
	Study and teaching
987	General works
988.A-Z	Individual schools, A-Z
	History and statistics
995	General works
	By period
996	Ancient
996.4	Medieval
	Modern see CD995
	Biography of archivists

	Archives
	History and statistics
	Biography of archivists -- Continued
997.A1	Collective
997.A2-Z	Individual, A-Z
	e.g.
997.F6	Finot
997.G3	Gaillard
	By region or country
	Europe
1000	Periodicals. Societies. Serials
1001	General works
1002	General inventories
1005	Family archives (General)
1010	Eastern Europe (General)
	Great Britain
	England and Wales (and Great Britain in general)
	Class here calendars and inventories of post-ca. 1800 official records
	For calendars and inventories of pre-ca. 1800 official records see DA25.C1
1040	Periodicals. Societies. Serials. Directories
1041	General works. History and statistics
1042	Inventories (General)
1042.A2	Bibliography or lists of inventories
	Subarrange by author, A-Z
	National archives
	Including national and other government archives combined
	At the capital city (or the central archives)
	History and description
1043.A1-.A3	Through 1850
1043.A4-Z	1851-1950
1043.3	1950-
1044	Nonofficial
	Including miscellaneous pamphlets
1045	Regulations
	For general discussions or organization see CD1043.A1+
1046	Inventories (General). By date
1047.A-Z	Special collections, A-Z
	Subarrange by date
1048.A-Z	Special class. By region or country, A-Z
	Special class. By subject
	see bibliography of subject in classes K, M, or Z
1049.A-Z	In places other than the capital, A-Z

Archives
  History and statistics
    By region or country
      Europe
        Great Britain
          England and Wales (and Great Britain in general)
            National archives -- Continued
              Other national government records by ministry, office, etc.

1051	Home Department. Foreign and Commonwealth Office (Table C4)
1051.5	Police (Table C4)
1052	Colonial Office (Table C4)
1052.5	Cabinet Office (Table C4)
1053	Admiralty (Table C4)
1053.5	Lord Chancellor's Dept. (Table C4)
1054	Defense (Table C4)
1054.5	Intelligence (Table C4)
1054.6	Tithe Commissioners (Table C4)
1055	Treasury (Table C4)
1055.5	Mint (Table C4)
1056	Exchequer and Audit (Table C4)
1057	Board of Trade (Table C4)
1057.5	Post Office (Table C4)
1058	Customs and Excise (Table C4)
1059	Paymaster General's (Table C4)
1060	Privy Council (Table C4)
1060.5	Health and Social Security (Table C4)
1061	Commisioner of Works (Table C4)
1061.5	Lord Steward's Dept. (Table C4)
1062	Population Censuses and Surveys (Table C4)
1063	Parliament (Table C4)
	Other local archives
1064	General local (divisions treated collectively)
1065.A-Z	Provincial, A-Z
	Local (municipal, communal, etc.) treated collectively
1066.A1	General works
1066.A2	General special. Probate, etc.
1066.A4-Z	By province (or other division), A-Z
	Subarrange by author
1067.A-Z	Municipal, A-Z
	Including notarial archives
	Parish registers
	Cf. CS434+ Genealogy
1068.A2	General works

Archives

  History and statistics

    By region or country

      Europe

        Great Britain

          England and Wales (and Great Britain in general)

           Parish registers -- Continued

1068.A3-Z	By county (or diocese) and parish, A-Z
	Under each county (or diocese):
	.x *General works*
	.x2A-.x2Z *By parish, A-Z*
1069.A-Z	Religious and academic institutions. By place, A-Z
	Other institutions
	see bibliography of subject in classes K, M, or Z
	Family archives
1069.5.A1	Collective
1069.5.A3-Z	Individual families, A-Z
	Subarrange each by author
1070-1099.5	Scotland (Table C1)
1100-1199.5	Ireland (Table C2)
1120-1149.5	Austria (Table C1 modified)
1120	Periodicals. Societies. Serials. Directories
1121	General works. History and statistics
1122	Inventories (General)
1122.A2	Bibliography or lists of inventories
	Subarrange by author, A-Z
	National archives
	Including national and other government archives
	combined
	At the capital city (or the central archives)
1123	History and description
1124	Nonofficial
	Including miscellaneous pamphlets
1125	Regulations
	For general discussions or organization see
	CD1123
1126	Inventories (General). By date
1127.A-Z	Special collections, A-Z
	Subarrange by date
1128.A-Z	Special class. By region or country, A-Z
	Special class. By subject
	see bibliography of subject in classes K, M, or Z
1129.A-Z	In places other than the capital, A-Z
	Other national government records, by ministry,
	office, etc.
1131	Foreign affairs (Table C4)
1132	Defense (Table C4)

Archives
　History and statistics
　　By region or country
　　　Europe
　　　　Austria
　　　　　National archives
　　　　　　Other national government records, by ministry, office, etc. -- Continued

1133	Navy (Table C4)
1143	Heads of state. Presidents. Prime ministers

　　　　　　　　For indexes to the manuscript papers of individual heads of state, see Z6616
　　　　　　　　For official documents of a head of a state, see class J
　　　　　　　　For the collected papers of individual heads of state, see classes D-F

1143.5	Parliament. Legislative Branch
	Other local archives
1144	General local (divisions treated collectively)
1145.A-Z	Provincial, A-Z
	Local (municipal, communal, etc.) treated collectively
1146.A1	General works
1146.A2	General special. Probate, etc.
1146.A4-Z	By province (or other division), A-Z
	Subarrange by author
1147.A-Z	Municipal, A-Z
	Including notarial archives
	Parish registers
1148.A1	Collective
1148.A2A-.A2Z	By diocese, parish, or other division, A-Z
1149.A-Z	Religious and academic institutions. By place, A-Z
	Other institutions
	see bibliography of subject in classes K, M, or Z
	Family archives
1149.5.A1	Collective
1149.5.A3-Z	Individual families, A-Z
	Subarrange each by author
1150-1169.5	Czechoslovakia. Czech Republic (Table C2)
1169.6	Slovakia
1170-1189.5	Hungary (Table C2)
	France
1190	Periodicals. Societies. Serials. Directories
1191	General works. History and statistics
1192	Inventories (General)
1192.A2	Bibliography of lists of inventories
	Subarrange by author, A-Z

	Archives
	History and statistics
	By region or country
	Europe
	France -- Continued
	National archives
	Including national and other government archives combined
	At the capital city (or the central archives)
1193	History and description
1194	Nonofficial
	Including miscellaneous pamphlets
1195	Regulations
	For general discussion on organization see CD1193
1196	Inventories (General). By date
1197.A-Z	Special collections, A-Z
	Subarrange by date
1198.A-Z	Special class. By region or country, A-Z
	Special class. By subject
	see bibliography of the subject in classes K, M, or Z
1199.A-Z	In places other than the capital, A-Z
	Other national government records, by ministry, office, etc.
1201	Foreign affairs (Table C4)
1202	Agriculture (Table C4)
1203	Colonies (Table C4)
1204	Commerce (Table C4)
1205	Finance (Table C4)
1206	Defense (Table C4)
1207	Education (Table C4)
1208	Interior (Table C4)
1209	Justice (Table C4)
1210	Marine (Table C4)
1211	Public works (Table C4)
1213.A-Z	Bureaus, A-Z
1213.5	Parliament. Legislative branch
	Local archives
	Including departments treated collectively
1214	General works
1215.A-Z	Departments, A-Z
1216.A-Z	Other divisions (except communes), A-Z
1217.A-Z	Communes, municipalities, etc., A-Z
	Religious and academic institutions
1218.A2	Collective
1218.A3-Z	By place, A-Z

	Archives
	History and statistics
	By region or country
	Europe
	France -- Continued
	Other institutions
	see bibliography of subject in classes K, M, or Z
	Family archives
1219.5.A1	Collective
1219.5.A3-Z	Individual families, A-Z
	Subarrange each by author
1220-1243.5	Germany (Table C1a modified)
	Including West Germany
	Other local archives
(1244)	General local (divisions treated collectively)
	This number is not used
1250-1274	Prussia (Table C1a)
1280-1304	Lower Saxony (Table C1a)
1310-1334	Bavaria (Table C1a)
1340-1364	Baden-Württemberg (Table C1a)
1373.A-Z	Other states and provinces, A-Z
	Local (municipal, etc.) treated collectively
1374.A1	General works
1374.A2	General special. Probate, etc.
	Subarrange by date (of first part if there are several)
1374.A4-Z	By province (or other division), A-Z
	Subarrange by date (of first part if there are several)
1375.A-Z	Municipal, A-Z
	Parish registers
1376	Collective
1376.5.A-Z	By diocese, parish, or other division, A-Z
	Religious and academic institutions
1377.A2	Collective
1377.A3-Z	By place, A-Z
	Other institutions
	see bibliography of subject in classes K, M, or Z
	Family archives
1377.5.A1	Collective
1377.5.A3-Z	Individual families, A-Z
	Each subarrange by author
	East Germany
1377.95	Periodicals. Societies. Serials. Directories
1377.951	General works. History and statistics
1377.952	Inventories (General)
1377.952.A2	Bibliography or lists of inventories
	Subarrange by author, A-Z

	Archives
	History and statistics
	By region or country
	Europe
	East Germany -- Continued
	National archives
	Including national and other government archives combined
	At the capital city (or the central archives)
1377.953	History and description
1377.954	Nonofficial
	Including miscellaneous pamphlets
1377.955	Regulations
	For general discussions on organization see CD1377.953
1377.956	Inventories (General). By date
1377.957.A-Z	Special collections, A-Z
	Subarrange by date
1377.958.A-Z	Special class. By region or country, A-Z
	Special class. By subject
	see bibliography of subject in classes K, M, or Z
1377.959.A-Z	In places other than the capital, A-Z
	Other national government records
1378.12	Defense
1378.135	Literature and the arts. Culture
1378.15	Treasury
1378.1525	Heads of state. Presidents. Prime ministers
	For indexes to the manuscript papers of individual heads of state, see Z6616
	For official documents of a head of a state, see class J
	For the collected papers of individual heads of state, see classes D-F
1378.155	Parliament. Legislative Branch
	Other local archives
1378.16	General local (divisions treated collectively)
1378.17.A-Z	Provincial, A-Z
	Local (municipal, communal, etc.) treated collectively
1378.175.A1	General works
1378.175.A2	General special. Probate, etc.
1378.175.A4-Z	By province (or other division), A-Z
	Subarrange by author
1378.18.A-Z	Municipal, A-Z
	Including notarial archives
	Parish registers
1378.185.A1	Collective

Archives
  History and statistics
    By region or country
      Europe
        East Germany
          Parish registers -- Continued

1378.185.A2A-.A2Z	By diocese, parish, or other division, A-Z
1378.19.A-Z	Religious and academic institutions. By place, A-Z
	Other institutions
	see bibliography of subject in classes K, M, or Z
	Family archives
1378.195.A1	Collective
1378.195.A3-Z	Individual families, A-Z
	Subarrange each by author
1380-1399.5	Greece (Table C2)
1400-1424	Italy (Table C1a)
1430-1454	Piedmont (Table C1a)
1460-1484	Liguria (Table C1a)
1490-1514	Lombardy (Table C1a)
1520-1544	Venetia (Table C1a)
1550-1574	Tuscany (Table C1a)
1580-1599.5	Papal States and Vatican (Table C2)
1600-1624	Campania (Table C1a)
1630-1646	Sicily (Table C2a)
1653.A-Z	Other regions, A-Z
1655.A-Z	Municipal, A-Z
	Parish registers
1656.A1	Collective
1656.A2-Z	By diocese, parish, or other division, A-Z
1657.A-Z	Religious and academic institutions. By place, A-Z
	Other institutions
	see bibliography of subject, in classes K, M, or Z
	Family archives
1658.A1	Collective
1658.A3-Z	Individual, A-Z
	Each subarrange by author
1670-1689.5	Belgium (Table C2)
1690-1709.5	Netherlands (Table C2)
	Russia. Soviet Union. Russia (Federation)
1710	Periodicals. Societies. Serials. Directories
1711	General works. History and statistics
1712	Inventories (General)
1712.A2	Bibliography or lists of inventories
	Subarrange by author, A-Z
	National archives
	Including national and other government archives
	combined

Archives
  History and statistics
    By region or country
     Europe
      Russia. Soviet Union. Russia (Federation)
       National archives -- Continued
        At the capital city (or the central archives)

1713	History and description
1714	Nonofficial
	Including miscellaneous pamphlets
1715	Regulations
	For general discussions on organization see CD1713
1716	Inventories (General). By date
1717.A-Z	Special collections, A-Z
	Subarrange by date
1718.A-Z	Special class. By region or country, A-Z
	Special class. By subject
	see bibliography of subject in classes K, M, or Z
1719.A-Z	In places other than the capital, A-Z
	Other national government records, by ministry, office, etc.
1721	Agriculture and land (Table C4)
1723	Communications and transport (Table C4)
1724	Council of ministers (Table C4)
1725	Finance (Table C4)
1726	Foreign affairs (Table C4)
1728	Interior (Table C4)
1728.5	Justice (Table C4)
1729	Navy (Table C4)
1730	Education (Table C4)
1731	Senate (Table C4)
1732	Defense. Military archives of the General Staff (Table C4)
1733	Literature and the arts
1733.2	Science and technology
1733.3	History. Central Party Archives
	Other local archives
1734	General local (divisions treated collectively)
1735.A-Z	Provincial, A-Z
	Local (municipal, communal, etc.) treated collectively
1736.A1	General works
1736.A2	General special. Probate, etc.
1736.A4-Z	By province (or other division), A-Z
	Subarrange by author

Archives
  History and statistics
    By region or country
      Europe
        Soviet Union
          Other local archives -- Continued

1737.A-Z	Municipal, A-Z
	Including notarial archives
	Parish registers
1738.A1	Collective
1738.A2A-.A2Z	By diocese, parish, or other division, A-Z
1739.A-Z	Religious and academic institutions. By place, A-Z
	Other institutions
	see bibliography of subject in classes K, M, or Z
	Family archives
1739.5.A1	Collective
1739.5.A3-Z	Individual families, A-Z
	Subarrange each by author
1739.6	Ukraine
1739.7	Belarus
1740-1759.5	Poland (Table C2)
	Baltic countries
1759.6	Estonia
1759.7	Latvia
1759.8	Lithuania
	Scandinavia
1760	General works
1770-1789.5	Denmark (Table C2)
1790-1809.5	Iceland (Table C2)
1810-1829.5	Norway (Table C2)
1830-1849.5	Sweden (Table C2)
1850-1879.5	Spain (Table C1)
1880-1899.5	Portugal (Table C2)
1900-1929.5	Switzerland (Table C1)
	Balkan States
1930	General works
1940-1949.5	Albania (Table C3)
1949.6	Bosnia and Hercegovina
1950-1959.5	Bulgaria (Table C3)
1960-1969.5	Croatia (Table C3)
1969.6	Macedonia (Republic)
1970-1979.5	Romania (Table C3)
1979.6	Slovenia
1980-1989.5	Yugoslavia (Table C3)
2000.A-Z	Other European, A-Z
	e.g.
2000.F5	Finland

	Archives
	History and statistics
	By region or country
	Europe
	Other European, A-Z -- Continued
2000.L8	Luxembourg
	Asia
2001	Periodicals. Societies. Serials
2002	General works
2003	General inventories
2010-2019.5	Israel. Palestine (Table C3)
2020-2029.5	Saudi Arabia (Table C3)
2030-2059.5	China (Table C1)
2060-2079.5	Indonesia (Table C2)
2080-2099.5	India (Table C2)
2099.6	Portuguese in India
2099.7	French in India
2100-2109.5	Pakistan (Table C3)
2120-2139.5	Vietnam (Table C2)
2140-2159.5	Thailand (Table C2)
2160-2189.5	Japan (Table C1)
2190-2209.5	Iran (Table C2)
2210-2239.5	Philippines (Table C1)
2250-2259.5	Korea (Table C3)
2260-2279.5	Turkey (Table C2)
2291.A-Z	Other Asian, A-Z
2291.A75	Armenia
2291.A76	Armenia (Republic)
2291.B26	Bahrain
2291.B35	Bangladesh
2291.B87	Burma. Myanmar
	Ceylon see CD2291.S7
2291.I54	Indochina
2291.K39	Kazakhstan
(2291.K6)	Korea
	see CD2250+
2291.K85	Kyrgyzstan
2291.M34	Malaysia
	Myanmar see CD2291.B87
2291.N4	Nepal
2291.P34	Papua New Guinea
2291.S55	Singapore
2291.S7	Sri Lanka
2291.T34	Taiwan
2291.T93	Turkmenistan
	Arab countries (General)
2295	Periodicals. Societies. Serials

	Archives
	History and statistics
	By region or country
	Arab countries (General) -- Continued
2295.2	General works
2295.3	General inventories
	Africa
2300	Periodicals. Societies. Serials
2301	General works
2302	General inventories
2310-2319.5	Algeria (Table C3)
2320-2329.5	Zaire (Table C3)
2330-2339.5	Egypt (Table C3)
2340-2349.5	Ethiopia (Table C3)
2350-2359.5	Ghana (Table C3)
2360-2369.5	Kenya (Table C3)
2370-2379.5	Liberia (Table C3)
2380-2389.5	Libya (Table C3)
2390-2399.5	Madagascar (Table C3)
2400-2409.5	Mauritius (Table C3)
2410-2419.5	Morocco (Table C3)
2420-2429.5	Nigeria (Table C3)
2430-2439.5	Zimbabwe (Table C3)
2440-2449.5	Sierra Leone (Table C3)
2450-2459.5	South Africa (Table C3)
2460-2469.5	Sudan (Table C3)
2470-2479.5	Tunisia (Table C3)
2480-2489.5	Tanzania (Table C3)
2491.A-Z	Other African, A-Z
2500-2529.5	Australia (Table C1)
2570-2789.5	New Zealand (Table C2)
	Pacific islands
2790	General works
2791	General inventories
2795.A-Z	Individual islands or groups or islands, A-Z
	America
	North America
	Cf. E97.9 Indian archives
3000	Periodicals. Societies. Serials
3001	General works
3002	General inventories
	United States
3020	Periodicals. Societies. Serials. Directories
3021	General works. History and statistics
3022	Inventories (General)
3022.A2	Bibliography or lists of inventories
	Subarrange by author, A-Z

Archives
  History and statistics
    By region or country
      America
        North America
          United States -- Continued
            National archives
              Including national and other government archives
                combined
              At the capital city (or the central archive)
3023   Documents of general character
                    e. g.
3023.A3   Annual report of the archivist
3024   Nonofficial
                    Including miscellaneous pamphlets
3025   Regulations
3026   Inventories (General). By date
3027.A-Z   Special collections, A-Z
                    Subarrange by date
3028.A-Z   Special class. By region or country, A-Z
                  Special class. By subject
                    see bibliogrpahy of subject in classes K, M, or Z
3029.A-Z   In places other than the capital, A-Z
                Family archives
3029.5.A1   General works
3029.5.A3-Z   Individual families
                    Subarrange each family by author
                Lists of papers of individuals see Z6616.A3+
                Executive Branch
                  Presidential papers
                    For the collected papers of individual presidents,
                      see class E, e.g. E302.M19 Madison papers
                    For Presidential messages issued as official
                      documents see J80+
                    For works about official Presidential
                      messages see JK587
                    For Presidential messages issues as official
                      documents see KF70.A5
                    For indexes to the manuscript papers of
                      individual presidents see Z6616.A3+
3029.8   General (Table C4)
3029.82   Presidential libraries (General) (Table C4)
                    For individual libraries, see the collected papers
                      of individual presidents in class E, e.g.
                      E838.5.K49 John Fitzgerald Kennedy
                      Library, Cambridge, Mass.
3030   General departmental (Table C4)

	Archives
	History and statistics
	By region or country
	America
	North America
	United States
	Executive Branch -- Continued
3031	State (Table C4)
3032	Treasury (Table C4)
3033	Defense (Table C4)
3034	Navy (Table C4)
3034.5	Air Force (Table C4)
3035	Interior (Table C4)
3036	Postal Service (Table C4)
3037	Justice (Table C4)
3038	Agriculture (Table C4)
3039	Commerce (Table C4)
3040	Labor (Table C4)
3040.4	Health, Education and Welfare (Table C4)
3041.A-Z	Other, A-Z (Table C4)
	Legislative Branch
3042	General works (Table C4)
3043	Congressmen. Senators (Collective) (Table C4)
	Cf. Z6616.A3+ Individual archives
	By period
3045	Colonial
3046	Revolution
3046.5	1789-1860
3047	Civil War
3047.5	1865-1898
3048	Spanish-American War
3049	1900-
3050	General local
	By section
3051	New England
3052	Atlantic States
3053	South
3054	Central States
3055	Lake region
	Mississippi Valley and West
3056	General works
3057	Southwest
3058	Northwest and Rocky Mountains
3059	Pacific Coast
3065	Religious and academic institutions (General)
	For individual archives, see subdivision (9) under the
	state in which the archive is located

	Archives
	History and statistics
	By region or country
	America
	North America
	United States -- Continued
	Other institutions
	see bibliography of subject in classes K, M, or Z
	By state
3070-3079	Alabama (Table C31)
3080-3089	Alaska (Table C31)
3090-3099	Arizona (Table C31)
3100-3109	Arkansas (Table C31)
3110-3119	California (Table C31)
3130-3139	Colorado (Table C31)
3140-3149	Connecticut (Table C31)
3150-3159	Delaware (Table C31)
3160-3169	District of Columbia (Table C31)
3170-3179	Florida (Table C31)
3180-3189	Georgia (Table C31)
	Hawaii
3189.1	Periodicals. Societies. Serials
3189.11	General history and statistics
3189.14	State archives
3189.16.A-Z	State departments, A-Z
3189.165	Legislative Branch (Table C4)
	Counties, A-Z
3189.17.A1	General works
3189.17.A2-Z	By county, A-Z
3189.18.A-Z	Municipal, A-Z
3189.19.A-Z	Religious and academic institutions. By place, A-Z
3190-3199	Idaho (Table C31)
3200-3209	Illinois (Table C31)
3220-3229	Indiana (Table C31)
3230-3239	Iowa (Table C31)
3240-3249	Kansas (Table C31)
3250-3259	Kentucky (Table C31)
3260-3269	Louisiana (Table C31)
3270-3279	Maine (Table C31)
3280-3289	Maryland (Table C31)
3290-3299	Massachusetts (Table C31)
3300-3309	Michigan (Table C31)
3310-3319	Minnesota (Table C31)
3320-3329	Mississippi (Table C31)
3330-3339	Missouri (Table C31)
3340-3349	Montana (Table C31)

Archives
  History and statistics
   By region or country
    America
     North America
      United States
       By state -- Continued

3350-3359	Nebraska (Table C31)
3360-3369	Nevada (Table C31)
3370-3379	New Hampshire (Table C31)
3380-3389	New Jersey (Table C31)
3390-3399	New Mexico (Table C31)
3400-3409	New York (Table C31)
3420-3429	North Carolina (Table C31)
3430-3439	North Dakota (Table C31)
3440-3449	Ohio (Table C31)
3450-3459	Oklahoma (Table C31)
3460-3469	Oregon (Table C31)
3470-3479	Pennsylvania (Table C31)
3480-3489	Rhode Island (Table C31)
3500-3509	South Carolina (Table C31)
3510-3519	South Dakota (Table C31)
3520-3529	Tennessee (Table C31)
3530-3539	Texas (Table C31)
3540-3549	Utah (Table C31)
3550-3559	Vermont (Table C31)
3560-3569	Virginia (Table C31)
3570-3579	Washington (Table C31)
3580-3589	West Virginia (Table C31)
3590-3599	Wisconsin (Table C31)
3600-3609	Wyoming (Table C31)
3615	United States insular possessions treated collectively
3620-3649.5	Canada (Table C1)
3649.8	Saint Pierre and Miquelon
3650-3679.5	Mexico (Table C1)

    Latin America

3680	Periodicals. Societies. Serials. Directories
3681	General works. History and statistics
3682	Inventories (General)
3682.A2	Bibliography or lists of inventories
	Subarrange by author, A-Z

     Central America

3690	Periodicals. Societies. Serials. Directories
3691	General works. History and description
3692	Inventories (General)

	Archives
	History and statistics
	By region or country
	America
	Latin America
	Central America
	Inventories (General) -- Continued
3692.A2	Bibliography or lists of inventories
	Subarrange by author, A-Z
3720-3739.5	Belize (Table C2)
3740-3759.5	Costa Rica (Table C2)
3760-3779.5	Guatemala (Table C2)
3780-3799.5	Honduras (Table C2)
3800-3819.5	Nicaragua (Table C2)
3820-3839.5	Panama (Table C2)
3840-3859.5	El Salvador (Table C2)
	West Indies
3860	Periodicals. Societies. Serials. Directories
3861	General works. History and statistics
3862	Inventories (General)
3862.A2	Bibliography or lists of inventories
	Subarrange by author, A-Z
3880-3899.5	Bahamas (Table C2)
3900-3919.5	Cuba (Table C2)
3920-3939.5	Haiti (Table C2)
3940-3959.5	Jamaica (Table C2)
3960-3979.5	Puerto Rico (Table C2)
3985.A-Z	Other, A-Z
	South America
4000	Periodicals. Societies. Serials. Directories
4001	General works. History and statistics
4002	Inventories (General)
4002.A2	Bibliography or lists of inventories
	Subarrange by author, A-Z
4020-4039.5	Argentina (Table C2)
4040-4059.5	Bolivia (Table C2)
4060-4079.5	Brazil (Table C2)
4080-4099.5	Chile (Table C2)
4100-4119.5	Colombia (Table C2)
4120-4139.5	Ecuador (Table C2)
4140-4159.5	Guyana (Table C2)
4160-4179.5	French Guiana (Table C2)
4180-4199.5	Suriname (Table C2)
4200-4219.5	Paraguay (Table C2)
4220-4239.5	Peru (Table C2)
4240-4259.5	Uruguay (Table C2)
4260-4279.5	Venezuela (Table C2)

	Archives	
	History and statistics	
	By region or country	
	America	
	Latin America	
	South America -- Continued	
4280.A-Z	South Atlantic islands, A-Z	
	Seals	
	Cf. CR101+ Standards, flags, banners	
	Cf. CR191+ Public and official heraldry	
	Cf. JC345+ Symbolism, emblems of the State	
5001	Periodicals. Serials	
5005	Societies	
5009	Congresses	
(5011)	Yearbooks	
	see CD5001	
	Collected works (nonserial)	
5013	Several authors	
5014	Individual authors	
	Exhibitions	
5017	International. By date	
5018.A-Z	Other. By place, A-Z	
	Museums	
	Public	
5019	General works	
5020.A-Z	By region or country, A-Z	

Under each country:

.x	General works
.x2A-.x2Z	Special. By city, A-Z

	Private	
5021	General works	
5022.A-Z	By region or country, A-Z	

Under each country:

.x	General works
.x2A-.x2Z	By collector, A-Z

5025	Sales catalogs
5027	Specimens
	Philosophy. Theory
5029	General works
5033	Relation to art
5035	Relation to diplomatics
5037	Relation to heraldry
5039	Relation to history
5041	Relation to numismatics
5045	Study and teaching
5049	History of sphragistics
	Biography

	Seals
	Biography -- Continued
5051	Collective
5052.A-Z	Individual, A-Z
5053	Directories
	Dictionaries. Encyclopedias
5055	General works
5057	Terminology
	General works
5059	Through 1800
	1801-
5061	American and English
5062	French
5063	German
5065	Other (not A-Z)
5073	Handbooks, manuals, etc.
5079	General special
	Execution. Technique
5085	General works
	Seal (the instrument)
5091	General works
5093	Matrix, stamp
5095	Signet, cachet, etc.
	Seal (the impression)
5101	General works
	Material
5111	General works
5113	Gold, silver
5114	Lead
5118	Wax
5122	Wafer
5126	Paper
	Form
5130	General works
5131	Round
5132	Oval
5133	Octagonal
5134	Lozenge
5139	Counter seal
5140	Color
	Attachment
5150	General works
5152	Plaque
	Pendant
5153	General works
5156	By strip of parchment
5157	Silk ribbon

	Seals
	Execution. Technique
	Seal (the impression)
	Attachment
	Pendant -- Continued
5158	Colored cord or thread
5159	Leather
5160	Single or double strip
	Inscriptions
5170	General works
5173	Figures, symbols, emblems
5174	Legend
5175	Date
5191	Iconography
	Ancient
5201	Periodicals. Societies. Serials
	Collected works (nonserial)
5204	Several authors
5205	Individual authors
	Exhibitions
5207	International. By date
5208.A-Z	Other. By place, A-Z
	Museums
	Public
5209	General works
5210.A-Z	By region or country, A-Z
	Under each country:
	.x *General works*
	Special. By city, A-Z
	Private
5211	General works
5212.A-Z	By region or country, A-Z
	Under each country:
	.x *General works*
	By collector, A-Z
5215	Sales catalogs
5219	Dictionaries. Encyclopedias
5221	General works
5225	Handbooks, manuals, etc.
5231	General special
5241	Iconography
	By country or people
5344	Middle East
	Including individual countries or peoples not otherwise provided for
5345	Egypt
5348	Assyria and Babylonia

	Seals
	Ancient
	By country or people -- Continued
5351	Phenicians
5354	Hebrews
5357	Hittites
5363	Crete
5369	Greeks
5373	Etruscans
	Romans
5375	General works
5377.A-Z	Special, A-Z
5381	Byzantine Empire
5383	India
5385	China
5391	Other (not A-Z)
	Medieval
5501	Periodicals. Societies. Serials
5505	Dictionaries. Encyclopedias
5507	General works
5513	General special
5525	Iconography
5535	Earliest
	Crusades. Latin Orient
5539	General works
	Military religious orders
5545	General works
5547	Knights of Malta
5549	Templars
5551	Teutonic Knights
5557.A-Z	By region or country, A-Z
5561	Renaissance
	For individual countries see CD5592.1+
	Modern
	General works see CD5001+
5575	16th-17th centuries
5577	18th century
5578	19th century
5579	20th century
	By region or country
5592.1-.95	North America (Table C7 modified)
	Add table number to CD5592
(5592.95.A-Z)	Local, A-Z
	see CD5601+
5601-5619	United States (Table C5 modified)
5617.A-Z	By region, A-Z
5617.N4	New England

	Seals
	Modern
	By region or country
	North America -- Continued
5619.1-.95	Canada (Table C7)
	Add table number to CD5619
5620.1-.95	Mexico (Table C7)
	Add table number to CD5620
5621-5630	Central America (Table C6 modified)
(5630.A-Z)	Local, A-Z
	see CD5631+
5631-5640	Belize (Table C6)
5641-5650	Costa Rica (Table C6)
5651-5660	Guatemala (Table C6)
5661-5670	Honduras (Table C6)
5671-5680	Nicaragua (Table C6)
5681-5690	Panama (Table C6)
5691-5700	El Salvador (Table C6)
5701-5710	West Indies (Table C6 modified)
(5710.A-Z)	Local, A-Z
	see CD5711+
5711-5720	Cuba (Table C6)
5721-5730	Haiti (Table C6)
5731-5740	Jamaica (Table C6)
5741.A-Z	Other, A-Z
5741.D6	Dominican Republic
5751-5760	South America (Table C6 modified)
(5760.A-Z)	Local, A-Z
	see CD5761+
5761-5770	Argentina (Table C6)
5771-5780	Bolivia (Table C6)
5781-5790	Brazil (Table C6)
5791-5800	Chile (Table C6)
5801-5810	Colombia (Table C6)
5811-5820	Ecuador (Table C6)
5821-5830	Guyana (Table C6)
5831-5840	Paraguay (Table C6)
5841-5850	Peru (Table C6)
5851-5860	Uruguay (Table C6)
5861-5870	Venezuela (Table C6)
5871-5880	Europe (Table C6 modified)
(5880.A-Z)	Local, A-Z
	see CD5881+
	Great Britain
5881	Periodicals. Societies. Serials
	Museums. Collections. Exhibitions
	Public

	Seals
	Modern
	By region or country
	Europe
	Great Britain
	Museums. Collections. Exhibitions
	Public -- Continued
5882	General works
5882.2.A-Z	By city, A-Z
	Private
5882.3	General works
5882.4.A-Z	By collector, A-Z
5883	General works
5884	General special
	Biography
5884.4	Collective
	For collections of the seals and designs of several artists see CD5883
5884.5.A-Z	Individual, A-Z

Under each:

.xA2	Autobiography. By date
.xA4	Reproductions (Collections). By date
.xA8-.xZ	Biography and criticism

Including collections of the seals and designs of individual artists

	By period
5886	Medieval and Renaissance
5887	Modern to 1800
5888	19th-20th centuries
	Special
5890	National, royal, etc.
5891	Companies, guilds
5892	Ecclesiastic, monastic, etc.
5893	Knighthood, orders, etc.
5894	Universities, colleges, schools (General)
	For individual institutions, see classes LD-LG
5895	Other institutional
5896.A-Z	Persons and families, other than royal, A-Z
5897.A-Z	Local, A-Z
5898	Wales
5899	Scotland
5899.1-.95	Ireland (Table C7)
	Add table number to CD5899
5901-5919	Austria (Table C5)
5919.1-.95	Hungary (Table C7)
	Add table number to CD5919

	Seals
	Modern
	By region or country
	Europe -- Continued
5921-5939	France (Table C5)
	Germany
	Including West Germany
5941	Periodicals. Societies. Serials
	Museums. Collections. Exhibitions
	Public
5942	General works
5942.2.A-Z	By city, A-Z
	Private
5942.3	General works
5942.4.A-Z	By collector, A-Z
5943	General works
5944	General special
	Biography
5944.4	Collective
	For collections of the seals and designs of several artists see CD5943
5944.5.A-Z	Individual, A-Z

Under each:

.xA2	*Autobiography. By date*
.xA4	*Reproductions (Collections). By date*
.xA8-.xZ	*Biography and criticism*

Including collections of the seals and designs of individual artists

	By period
5946	Medieval and Renaissance
5947	Modern to 1800
5948	19th-20th centuries
	Special
5949	Imperial, royal, etc.
5950	Companies, guilds
5951	Ecclesiastical, monastic, etc.
5952	Other institutional
5953.A-Z	Persons and families, other than royal, A-Z
	Local
5954	Baden-Württemberg
5955	Bavaria
5956	Prussia
5957	Lower Saxony
5958	North Rhine-Westphalia
5959.A-Z	Other states and provinces, A-Z
5960.A-Z	Cities and towns, A-Z

	Seals
	Modern
	By region or country
	Europe -- Continued
5960.2	East Germany
	Poland

5960.2 — East Germany
Poland

5960.51 — Periodicals. Societies. Serials
Museums. Collections. Exhibitions
Public

5960.52 — General works
5960.522.A-Z — By city, A-Z
Private
5960.523 — General works
5960.524.A-Z — By collector, A-Z
5960.53 — General works
5960.54 — General special
Biography
5960.544 — Collective

For collections of the seals and designs of
several artists see CD5960.53

5960.545.A-Z — Individual, A-Z
Under each:
.xA2   *Autobiography. By date*
.xA4   *Reproductions (Collections). By date*
.xA8-.xZ   *Biography and criticism*
Including collections of the seals and designs of
individual artists
By period
5960.55 — Medieval and Renaissance
5960.56 — Modern to 1800
5960.57 — 19th-20th centuries
5960.58 — Special
5960.59.A-Z — Persons and families, other than royal, A-Z
5960.595.A-Z — Local, A-Z
5961-5970 — Greece (Table C6)
5971-5989 — Italy (Table C5)
6001-6010 — Belgium (Table C6)
6011-6020 — Netherlands (Table C6)
6021-6030 — Russia. Former Soviet republics (Table C6)
6031-6040 — Scandinavia (Table C6 modified)
6040.A-Z — Local, A-Z
see CD6041+
6041-6050 — Denmark (Table C6)
6051-6060 — Iceland (Table C6)
6061-6070 — Norway (Table C6)
6071-6080 — Sweden (Table C6)

	Seals
	Modern
	By region or country
	Europe -- Continued
6081-6090	Spain (Table C6)
6091-6100	Portugal (Table C6)
6101-6110	Switzerland (Table C6)
6111-6120	Balkan States (Table C6 modified)
6120.A-Z	Local, A-Z
	see CD6121+
6121-6130	Bulgaria (Table C6)
6130.1-.95	Croatia (Table C7)
	Add table number to CD6130
6131-6140	Romania (Table C6)
6140.1-.95	Slovenia (Table C7)
6141-6150	Yugoslavia (Table C6)
6151.A-Z	Other European, A-Z
6151.L8	Luxembourg
6161-6170	Asia (Table C6 modified)
(6170.A-Z)	Local, A-Z
	see CD6171+
6171-6180	China (Table C6)
6181-6190	Indonesia (Table C6)
6191-6200	India (Table C6)
6201-6210	Southeast Asia (Table C6)
6221-6220	Thailand (Table C6)
6241-6250	Japan (Table C6)
6251-6260	Iran (Table C6)
6261-6270	Philippines (Table C6)
6271-6280	Turkey (Table C6)
6295.A-Z	Other Asian, A-Z
6301-6310	Africa (Table C6 modified)
(6310.A-Z)	Local, A-Z
	see CD6311+
6311-6320	Egypt (Table C6)
6365.A-Z	Other African, A-Z
6371-6389	Australia (Table C5)
6461-6470	New Zealand (Table C6)
6471.A-Z	Pacific islands, A-Z

CD

	Technical chronology. Calendar
	For historical chronology, see classes D - F
1	Periodicals. Societies. Serials
1.5	Congresses
	Collected works
2	Several authors
3	Individual authors
4	Dictionaries. Encyclopedias
	History
6	General works
	Biography
7	Collective
8.A-Z	Individual, A-Z
	e.g.
8.C5	Clinton, H.F.
	General works
10	Through 1800
11	1801-
12	General special
13	Juvenile works
15	Comparative chronology
	Primitive see GN476.3
	Ancient
21	General works
25	General special
29	Egyptian
	Asian
31	General works
33	Assyrian. Babylonian. Chaldean
34	Persian
35	Hebrew
	Including Hebrew and Islamic
36	Turkish
36.5	Armenian
37	Chinese
38	Japanese
38.5	Buddhist
38.7	Lamaist
39	Hindu
39.5	Bengali
40	Other special (not A-Z)
	For Mexican (Aztec) see F1219.3.C2
42	Greek
43	Minoan
46	Roman
	Medieval and modern
	Christian era

CE

	Medieval and modern
	Christian era -- Continued
51	General works
55	Other (not A-Z)
57	Medieval
59	Islamic
61.A-Z	By region or country, A-Z
73	Reform of the calendar
	Special systems
75	Julian
76	Gregorian
77	Republican (French)
	Church chronology, feast days, etc.
81	General works
83	Easter
85	Special topics (not A-Z)
	Including cycles, etc.
	Bible chronology see BS637+
89	Clog almanacs
	Perpetual calendars. Century calendars, etc.
91	General works
92	Popular works
97	Other material not elsewhere provided for
	Cf. N, Art calendars
	Cf. PN-PT, Literary calendars
	Cf. BV4810+ Christian devotional calendars
	Cf. ML12 Music calendars (International)
	Cf. ML13 Music calendars (U.S.)
	Cf. ML21.A+ Music calendars (Other)

	Numismatics
	Coins
	Class here works on the general subject of numismatics
	Cf. HG231+ History of money
	Periodicals. Serials. By language
1	English
3	French
5	German
9	Other (not A-Z)
	Societies
14	International
	By language
15	English
17	French
19	German
23	Other (not A-Z)
27	Congresses
(31)	Yearbooks
	see CJ1+
	Collected works (nonserial)
35	Several authors
36	Individual authors
	Exhibitions
39	International. By date
41	Other. By place, A-Z
	Museums. Collections
	Public
42	General works
43.A-Z	By region or country, A-Z

Under each country:

.x	*General works*
.x2A-.x2Z	*Special. By city, A-Z*

	Private
44	General works
45.A-Z	By region or country, A-Z

Under each country:

.x	*General works*
.x2A-.x2Z	*By collector, A-Z*

	Sales catalogs
47	Auction
49	Dealers'
53	Philosophy. Theory
55	Study and teaching
	History
59	General works
60.A-Z	By region or country, A-Z
	Biography

	Coins
	History
	Biography -- Continued
61	Collective
62.A-Z	Individual, A-Z
	e.g.
62.D8	Du Bois, W.E.
63	Directories
	Dictionaries. Encyclopedias
	Cf. CJ89 Coin encyclopedias
67	General works
69	Terminology
71	Abbreviations. Inscriptions
	For works limited to a specific period or country, see the period or country, CJ201+
	General works
73	Through 1800
75	1801-1970
76	1971-
81	Handbooks, manuals, etc.
89	Popular works. Coin encyclopedias
101	General special
	Including counterfeits and couterfeiters
	Coins of special materials (General)
	Including works on coin materials
	For works on coins of a particular country, see the country, CJ355+ CJ847+ etc.
109	General works
113	Gold
115	Silver
117	Bronze and copper
119	Other metals (not A-Z)
	Execution. Technique
125	General works
129	Coin types
151	Iconography
	Finds of coins
	For finds limited to a specific period or place of origin, see CJ275+ CJ391+ etc.
153.A2	General works
153.A3-Z	By place of discovery, A-Z
161.A-Z	Symbols, devices, etc.
161.A6	Animals
161.A72	Architecture
161.A75	Arms and armor. Weapons
161.A82	Astronomy
161.B7	Bridges

CJ

Coins

Symbols, devices, etc. -- Continued

161.C3	Castles
161.D6	Dollar sign
161.E5	Elephant
161.F3	Facing head
161.G6	Gods
161.H66	Horsemen and horsewomen
161.H67	Horses
161.K54	Kings and rulers
161.L56	Lions
161.M55	Mines and mineral resources
161.M8	Music
161.N3	Natural history
161.P35	Paintings
161.P65	Portrait sculpture
161.S5	Ships
161.S65	Sports
161.T48	Tetragrammaton
161.T73	Transportation
	Weapons see CJ161.A75
161.W56	Wine and wine making
161.W65	Women

Ancient

201	Periodicals. Societies. Serials
(205)	Yearbooks
	see CJ201
	Collected works (nonserial)
208	Several authors
209	Individual authors
	Exhibitions
211	International. By date
213.A-Z	Other. By place, A-Z
	Museums. Collections
	Public
214	General works
215.A-Z	By region or country, A-Z

Under each country:

.x	*General works*
.x2A-.x2Z	*Special. By city, A-Z*

Private

216	General works
217.A-Z	By region or country, A-Z

Under each country:

.x	*General works*
.x2A-.x2Z	*By collector, A-Z*

Sales catalogs

	Coins
	Ancient
	Sales catalogs -- Continued
219	Auction
221	Dealers'
223	Philosophy. Theory
229	Dictionaries. Encyclopedias
	General works
231	Through 1800
233	1801-
237	Handbooks, manuals, etc.
245	General special
255	Coins of the Bible
265	Iconography
	Finds of coins
	Cf. CJ391+ Greek
	Cf. CJ891+ Roman
275	General works
277.A-Z	By place of discovery, A-Z
	Greek
301	Periodicals. Societies. Serials
(305)	Yearbooks
	see CJ301
	Collected works (nonserial)
309	Several authors
310	Individual authors
	Exhibitions
311	International. By date
313.A-Z	Other. By place, A-Z
	Museums. Collections
	Public
314	General works
315.A-Z	By region or country, A-Z
	Under each country:
	.x *General works*
	.x2A-.x2Z *Special. By city, A-Z*
	Private
316	General works
317.A-Z	By region or country, A-Z
	Under each country:
	.x *General works*
	.x2A-.x2Z *By collector, A-Z*
	Sales catalogs
319	Auction
321	Dealers'
323	Philosophy. Theory
329	Dictionaries. Encyclopedias

CJ

Coins
  Ancient
    Greek -- Continued
      General works

333	Through 1800
335	1801-
339	Handbooks, manuals, etc.
351	General special
	Coins of special materials (General)
355	General works
357	Gold
359	Silver
361	Bronze and copper
363	Other metals (not A-Z)
	Execution. Technique
369	General works
373	Coin types
385	Iconography
	Finds of coins
391	General works
393.A-Z	By place of discovery, A-Z
	By period
401	Archaic, 700-480 B.C.
403	Transitional, 480-415 B.C.
405	Finest art, 415-336 B.C.
407	Later fine art, 336-280 B.C.
409	Decline, 280-146 B.C.
411	Later decline, 146-27 B.C.
413	Imperial period, 27 B.C.-268 A.D.
	By region or country
	Europe
425	General works
	Greece
427	General works
429	Northern
431	Central
433	Eastern
435	Southern
	Including Peloponnesus
437	Ionian Islands
439	Islands of the Aegean
	By state or island
	Acarnania
445	Catalogs and collections
446	Treatises
447.A-Z	Local, A-Z
	Aegina

CJ

Coins
  Ancient
    Greek
      By region or country
        Europe
          Italy
            Campania -- Continued
528.A-Z   Local, A-Z
            Etruria
529   General works
530.A-Z   Local, A-Z
            Latium
533   General works
534.A-Z   Local, A-Z
            Lucania
535   General works
536.A-Z   Local, A-Z
            Picenum
537   General works
538.A-Z   Local, A-Z
            Samnium
539   General works
540.A-Z   Local, A-Z
            Umbria
541   General works
542.A-Z   Local, A-Z
          Macedonia
            Including Alexander the Great
545   Catalogs and collections
546   Treatises
547.A-Z   Local, A-Z
          Northern Black Sea Region
548   General works
548.5.A-Z   Local, A-Z
          Sicily
            Including Syracuse and other local
549   General works
550.A-Z   Local, A-Z
          Malta, Gozo, and Pantelleria (Cossyra)
551   General works
552.A-Z   Local, A-Z
          Spain
553   Catalogs and collections
554   Treatises
555.A-Z   Local, A-Z
          Thrace
557   Catalogs and collections

	Coins
	Ancient
	Greek
	By region or country
	Europe
	Thrace -- Continued
558	Treatises
559.A-Z	Local, A-Z
	Asia
573	General works
	Asia Minor
575	General works
	Aeolis
577	Catalogs and collections
578	Treatises
579.A-Z	Local, A-Z
	Lesbos
581	Catalogs and collections
582	Treatises
583.A-Z	Local, A-Z
	Bithynia
585	Catalogs and collections
586	Treatises
587.A-Z	Local, A-Z
	Cappadocia
589	Catalogs and collections
590	Treatises
591.A-Z	Local, A-Z
	Caria
593	Catalogs and collections
594	Treatises
595.A-Z	Local, A-Z
	Cilicia
597	Catalogs and collections
598	Treatises
599.A-Z	Local, A-Z
	Galatia
601	Catalogs and collections
602	Treatises
603.A-Z	Local, A-Z
	Ionia
605	Catalogs and collections
606	Treatises
607.A-Z	Local, A-Z
	Lycaonia
609	Catalogs and collections
610	Treatises

Coins
  Ancient
    Greek
      By region or country
        Asia
          Asia Minor
            Lycaonia -- Continued

611.A-Z	Local, A-Z
	Lycia
613	Catalogs and collections
614	Treatises
615.A-Z	Local, A-Z
	Lydia
617	Catalogs and collections
618	Treatises
619.A-Z	Local, A-Z
	Mysia
621	Catalogs and collections
622	Treatises
623.A-Z	Local, A-Z
	Pamphylia
625	Catalogs and collections
626	Treatises
627.A-Z	Local, A-Z
	Paphlagonia
629	Catalogs and collections
630	Treatises
631.A-Z	Local, A-Z
	Phrygia
633	Catalogs and collections
634	Treatises
635.A-Z	Local, A-Z
	Pisidia
637	Catalogs and collections
638	Treatises
639.A-Z	Local, A-Z
	Pontus
641	Catalogs and collections
642	Treatises
643.A-Z	Local, A-Z
	Troas
645	Catalogs and collections
646	Treatises
647.A-Z	Local, A-Z
	Arabia
651	Catalogs and collections
652	Treatises

Coins
 Ancient
  Greek
   By region or country
    Asia -- Continued
     Persia

695	Catalogs and collections
696	Treatises
697.A-Z	Local, A-Z

     Syria

699	Catalogs and collections
700	Treatises
701.A-Z	Local, A-Z

      Palestine

705	Catalogs and collections
706	Treatises
707.A-Z	Local, A-Z

      Phenicia

709	Catalogs and collections
710	Treatises
711.A-Z	Local, A-Z

    Africa

725	General works

     Byzacium

729	Catalogs and collections
730	Treatises
731.A-Z	Local, A-Z

     Cyrenaica

733	Catalogs and collections
734	Treatises
735.A-Z	Local, A-Z

     Egypt

737	Catalogs and collections
738	Treatises
739.A-Z	Local, A-Z

     Ethiopia

741	Catalogs and collections
742	Treatises
743.A-Z	Local, A-Z

     Libya

745	Catalogs and collections
746	Treatises
747.A-Z	Local, A-Z

     Mauretania

749	Catalogs and collections
750	Treatises
751.A-Z	Local, A-Z

	Coins
	Ancient
	Greek
	By region or country
	Africa -- Continued
	Numidia
753	Catalogs and collections
754	Treatises
755.A-Z	Local, A-Z
	Syrtica
757	Catalogs and collections
758	Treatises
759.A-Z	Local, A-Z
	Zeugitana
761	Catalogs and collections
762	Treatises
763.A-Z	Local, A-Z
	Roman
801	Periodicals. Societies. Serials
(805)	Yearbooks
	see CJ801
	Collected works (nonserial)
809	Several authors
810	Individual authors
	Exhibitions
811	International. By date
813.A-Z	Other. By place, A-Z
	Museums. Collections
	Public
814	General works
815.A-Z	By region or country, A-Z
	Under each country:
	.x *General works*
	.x2A-.x2Z *Special. By city, A-Z*
	Private
816	General works
817.A-Z	By region or country, A-Z
	Under each country:
	.x *General works*
	.x2A-.x2Z *By collector, A-Z*
	Sales catalogs
819	Auction
821	Dealers'
823	Philosophy. Theory
829	Dictionaries. Encyclopedias
	General works
831	Through 1800

Coins

  Ancient

    Roman

      General works -- Continued

833	1801-
837	Handbooks, manuals, etc.
843	General special
	Coins of special materials (General)
847	General works
849	Gold
851	Silver
	Bronze, brass, and copper
853	General works
855	First brasses (large)
856	Second brasses (middle)
857	Third brasses (small)
859	Other metals (not A-Z)
	Execution. Technique
863	General works
865	Coin types
885	Iconography
	Finds of coins
891	General works
893.A-Z	By place of discovery, A-Z
	Republican
901	Collected works (nonserial)
905	Dictionaries. Encyclopedias
909	General works
915	General special
	Including material, technique, etc.
925	Iconography
	By period
	Early
935	General works
937	Heavy bronze. Aes grave
	Later
941	General works
943	National types
	Consular or family coins
	Museums and collections see CJ814+
	General works
946	Through 1800
947	1801-
949.A-Z	By family, A-Z
	Imperial
961	Collected works (nonserial)
965	Dictionaries. Encyclopedias

Coins
  Ancient
    Roman
      By region or province
        Italy
          Latium -- Continued

1051.A-Z	Local, A-Z
	Lucania
1053	Catalogs and collections
1054	Treatises
1055.A-Z	Local, A-Z
	Picenum
1057	Catalogs and collections
1058	Treatises
1059.A-Z	Local, A-Z
	Samnium
1061	Catalogs and collections
1062	Treatises
1063.A-Z	Local, A-Z
	Umbria
1065	Catalogs and collections
1066	Treatises
1067.A-Z	Local, A-Z
	Oscan coins
1068	Catalogs and collections
1069	Treatises
1070.A-Z	Local, A-Z
	Africa
	Egypt
1071	Catalogs and collections
1072	Treatises
1073.A-Z	Local, A-Z
	Africa (Province)
1075	Catalogs and collections
1076	Treatises
1077.A-Z	Local, A-Z
	Mauretania
1079	Catalogs and collections
1080	Treatises
1081.A-Z	Local, A-Z
	Numidia
1083	Catalogs and collections
1084	Treatises
1085.A-Z	Local, A-Z
	Asia
1087	Catalogs and collections
1088	Treatises

CJ

	Coins
	Ancient
	Roman
	By region or province
	Asia -- Continued
	Asia (Province)
1090	Catalogs and collections
1091	Treatises
1092.A-Z	Local, A-Z
	Syria
1093	Catalogs and collections
1094	Treatises
1095.A-Z	Local, A-Z
1099.A-Z	Other provinces, A-Z
	Europe
	Britain (Britannia)
1101	Catalogs and collections
1102	Treatises
1103.A-Z	Local, A-Z
	Dacia
1105	Catalogs and collections
1106	Treatises
1107.A-Z	Local, A-Z
	Dalmatia
1109	Catalogs and collections
1110	Treatises
1111.A-Z	Local, A-Z
	Gaul (Gallia)
	For pre-Roman period see CJ2681
1113	Catalogs and collections
1114	Treatises
1115.A-Z	Local, A-Z
	Germany (Germania)
1117	Catalogs and collections
1118	Treatises
1119.A-Z	Local, A-Z
	Iberia (Hispania)
1121	Catalogs and collections
1122	Treatises
1123.A-Z	Local, A-Z
	Illyria (Illyricum)
1125	Catalogs and collections
1126	Treatises
1127.A-Z	Local, A-Z
	Italy
	see CJ1021+
	Moesia

	Coins
	Ancient
	Roman
	By region or province
	Europe
	Moesia -- Continued
1129	Catalogs and collections
1130	Treatises
1131.A-Z	Local, A-Z
1132	Pannonia
	Sardinia
1133	Catalogs and collections
1134	Treatises
1135.A-Z	Local, A-Z
	Sicily (Sicilia)
1137	Catalogs and collections
1138	Treatises
1139.A-Z	Local, A-Z
	Thrace
1145	Catalogs and collections
1146	Treatises
1147.A-Z	Local, A-Z
	Byzantine
1201	Periodicals. Societies. Serials
	Collected works (nonserial)
1208	Several authors
1209	Individual authors
	Museums. Collections
	Public
1214	General works
1215.A-Z	By region or country, A-Z
	Under each country:
	.x *General works*
	.x2A-.x2Z *Special. By city, A-Z*
	Private
1216	General works
1217.A-Z	By region or country, A-Z
	Under each country:
	.x *General works*
	.x2A-.x2Z *By collector, A-Z*
	Sales catalogs
1219	Auction
1221	Dealers'
1227	Dictionaries. Encyclopedias
1229	General works
1235	Handbooks, manuals, etc.
1241	General special

CJ

	Coins
	Ancient
	African and Oriental
	By region or country
	Asia and Ancient Orient -- Continued
	General works see CJ1309
1361	Assyria
1363	Persia. Iran
1365	Babylonia
1367	China
1369	Egypt
1375	Jewish (and Samaritan). Palestine
1379	Phenicia. Tyre. Sidon
1381	Carthage
1391	India
1397	Other (not A-Z)
	Japan see CJ3700+
	Medieval and modern
	For Byzantine see CJ1201+
	Periodicals, societies, collected works, etc.
	see CJ1+
	Exhibitions
1509	International. By date
1511.A-Z	Other. By place, A-Z
	Museums. Collections
	Public
1512	General works
1513.A-Z	By region or country, A-Z
	Under each country:
	.x *General works*
	.x2A-.x2Z *Special. By city, A-Z*
	Private
1514	General works
1515.A-Z	By region or country, A-Z
	Under each country:
	.x *General works*
	.x2A-.x2Z *By collector, A-Z*
	Sales catalogs
1517	Auction
1519	Dealers'
	Philosophy. Theory see CJ53
1525	Dictionaries. Encyclopedias
	General works
1527	Through 1800
1529	1801-
1533	Handbooks, manuals, etc.

CJ

Coins
  Medieval and modern -- Continued
1539   General special
        Including obsidional coins
      Coins of special materials (General)
1543   General works
1545   Gold
1546   Silver
1547   Bronze and copper
1548   Other metals (not A-Z)
        Including nickel
      Execution. Technique
1557   General works
1559   Coin types
1575   Iconography
      By period
       Medieval
1601   Periodicals. Societies. Serials
1605   Dictionaries. Encyclopedias
1607   General works
1615   General special
         Including symbolism
        Coins of special materials (General)
1618   General works
1619   Gold
1620   Silver
1621   Bronze and copper
1622   Other metals (not A-Z)
        Execution. Technique
1625   General works
1627   Coin types
1637   Iconography
       Finds of coins
1645   General works
1647.A-Z   By place of discovery, A-Z
       Migrations
1657   General works
1661   Visigoths (and Goths in general)
1663   Ostrogoths
1664   Suevi
1665   Vandals
1667   Huns
1669   Lombards
1671   Normans
1673   Slavs
1675   Other special (not A-Z)
       Crusades. Latin Orient

	Coins
	Medieval and modern
	By region or country
	America
	United States -- Continued
1826	Sales catalogs
1829	Dictionaries. Directories
1830	General works
1832	General special
	Coins of special materials
1834	Gold
1835	Silver
1836	Bronze and copper
1837	Other (not A-Z)
	Commemorative and souvenir coins
1839	General works
1840.A-Z	Special. By name, A-Z
	e.g.
1840.M2	McKinley souvenir dollar
	By period
1841	Colonial
1842	Early national through 1860
1844	1861 through 1900
1845	1901-
	Local
1848.A-.W	States, A-W
1849.A-Z	Cities and towns, A-Z
1860-1879	Canada (Table C9)
	Latin America
1889	General works
1890-1909	Mexico (Table C9)
1910-1919	Central America (Table C9 modified)
(1919.A-Z)	Local, A-Z
	see CJ1930+
1930-1949	Belize (Table C9)
1950-1969	Costa Rica (Table C9)
1970-1989	Guatemala (Table C9)
1990-2009	Honduras (Table C9)
2010-2029	Nicaragua (Table C9)
2030-2049	Panama (Table C9)
2050-2069	El Salvador (Table C9)
2070-2089	West Indies (Table C9 modified)
(2089.A-Z)	Local, A-Z
	see CJ2090+
2090-2109	Bahamas (Table C9)
2110-2129	Cuba (Table C9)
2130-2149	Haiti (Table C9)

	Coins
	Medieval and modern
	By region or country
	America
	Latin America
	West Indies -- Continued
2150-2169	Jamaica (Table C9)
2170-2189	Puerto Rico (Table C9)
2195.A-Z	Other West Indian islands, A-Z
2200-2219	South America (Table C9 modified)
(2219.A-Z)	Local, A-Z
	see CJ2220+
2220-2239	Argentina (Table C9)
2240-2259	Bolivia (Table C9)
2260-2279	Brazil (Table C9)
2280-2299	Chile (Table C9)
2300-2319	Colombia (Table C9)
2320-2339	Ecuador (Table C9)
2340-2349	French Guiana (Table C10)
2350-2359	Guyana (Table C10)
2360-2379	Paraguay (Table C9)
2380-2399	Peru (Table C9)
2400-2409	Suriname (Table C10)
2410-2429	Uruguay (Table C9)
2430-2449	Venezuela (Table C9)
2450-2469	Europe (Table C9 modified)
(2469.A-Z)	Local, A-Z
	see CJ2470+
2469.5	Eastern Europe (General)
2470-2499	Great Britain. England
2470	Periodicals. Societies. Serials
(2471)	Yearbooks
	see CJ2470
2472	Collected works (nonserial)
	Museums. Collections. Exhibitions
	Public
2474	General works
2474.2.A-Z	By city, A-Z
	Private
2475	General works
2475.2.A-Z	By collector, A-Z
2476	Sales catalogs. Coin values
2479	Dictionaries. Directories
2480	General works
2482	General special
	Coins of special materials
2484	Gold

CJ

	Coins
	Medieval and modern
	By region or country
	Europe -- Continued
2870-2889	Greece (Table C9)
2900-2929	Italy (Table C8)
2930-2949	Low countries (Table C9 modified)
(2949.A-Z)	Local, A-Z
	see CJ2950+
2950-2969	Belgium (Table C9)
2970-2989	Netherlands (Table C9)
2990-2999	Luxembourg (Table C10)
(2999.5)	Eastern Europe
	see CJ2469
3000-3029	Russia (Table C8)
3029.5	Belarus
3029.7	Ukraine
3030-3049	Poland (Table C9)
3049.5	Baltic Sea Region
	Baltic countries
3050-3059	Estonia (Table C10)
3060-3069	Latvia (Table C10)
3070-3079	Lithuania (Table C10)
3080-3099	Scandinavia (Table C9 modified)
(3099.A-Z)	Local, A-Z
	see CJ3100+
3100-3119	Denmark (Table C9)
3120-3129	Finland (Table C10)
3130-3139	Iceland (Table C10)
3140-3159	Norway (Table C9)
3160-3179	Sweden (Table C9)
3180-3199	Spain (Table C9)
3199.5	Malta
3210-3229	Portugal (Table C9)
3240-3269	Switzerland (Table C8)
	Balkan States
3269.5	Albania
3270-3279	Bosnia and Hercegovina (Table C10)
3280-3289	Croatia (Table C10)
3290-3309	Bulgaria (Table C9)
3310-3319	Macedonia (Table C10)
3320-3329	Slovenia (Table C10)
3330-3349	Romania (Table C9)
3350-3369	Yugoslavia (Table C9)
3370-3389	Asia (Table C9 modified)
(3389.A-Z)	Local, A-Z
	see CJ3430+

	Coins
	Medieval and modern
	By region or country
	Asia -- Continued
3400-3429	Near East. Arab countries. Islamic Empire (Table C8 modified)
3413	Arabic glass weight for testing coins
	Local
(3428.A-Z)	States, provinces, etc., A-Z
	see CJ3430+
(3429.A-Z)	Cities and towns, A-Z
	see CJ3430+
3430-3449	Turkey (Table C9)
3455	Afghanistan
	Arabian Peninsula
3456	General works
3457	Saudi Arabia
3458	Persian Gulf States (Collectively). Trucial States (Collectively)
3459	Oman
3461	Kuwait
3463	Yemen
3481	Armenia
3482	Azerbaijan
3484	Georgia (Republic)
	Central Asia
3487	General works
3487.23	Kazakhstan
3487.24	Kyrgyzstan
3487.25	Tajikistan
3487.26	Turkmenistan
3487.27	Uzbekistan
	Far East
3488	General works
3490-3509	China (Table C9)
3510-3519	Tibet (Table C9)
3520-3529	Mongolia (Table C9)
3530-3549	India (Table C9)
3550-3559	Sri Lanka (Table C10)
3560-3569	Nepal (Table C10)
3570-3579	Burma. Myanmar (Table C10)
3580-3589	Cambodia (Table C10)
3590-3599	Vietnam (Table C10)
3600-3619	Thailand (Table C10)
3620-3629	Malaysia. Malay Peninsula (Table C10)
3640-3659	Indonesia (Table C9)
3660-3679	Philippines (Table C9)

CJ

	Coins
	Medieval and modern
	By region or country
	Asia
	Far East -- Continued
3700-3719	Japan (Table C9)
3730-3749	Korea (Table C9)
3750-3769	Iran (Table C9)
3770-3789	Iraq (Table C9)
3850-3869	Israel. Palestine (Table C9)
3870-3889	Syria (Table C9)
3891	Jordan
3893	Cyprus
3900-3919	Africa (Table C9 modified)
(3919.A-Z)	Local, A-Z
	see CJ3920+
3920-3929	Ethiopia (Table C9)
3940-3959	South Africa (Table C9)
3980	Namibia
4100	Zaire
4110	Tunisia
4120-4139	Egypt (Table C9)
4160-4179	Algeria (Table C9)
4187	Madagascar
4270-4289	Liberia (Table C9)
4290-4309	Morocco (Table C9)
4333	Mozambique
4335	Angola
4339	Sao Tome and Principe
4370-4389	Libya (Table C9)
	Indian Ocean islands
4393	General
4394.A-Z	Individual islands or groups of islands, A-Z
4394.R47	Réunion
4400-4419	Australia (Table C9)
4580-4599	New Zealand (Table C9)
	Pacific Islands
4600	General works
4625.A-Z	Individual islands and groups of islands, A-Z
	Hawaiian islands, see CJ1848.H3
	Tokens
4801	Periodicals. Societies. Serials
	Collected works (nonserial)
4803	Several authors
4804	Individual authors
	Museums. Collections
	Public

	Tokens
	Museums. Collections
	Public -- Continued
4805	General works
4806.A-Z	By region or country, A-Z

Under each country:

.x	*General works*
.x2A-.x2Z	*Special. By city, A-Z*

	Private
4807	General works
4808.A-Z	By region or country, A-Z

Under each country:

.x	*General works*
.x2A-.x2Z	*By collector, A-Z*

4809	Sales catalogs
4813	Dictionaries. Encyclopedias
4815	General works
4819	General special
4825.A-Z	Special tokens. By form, A-Z
	By period
	Ancient
4861	General works
4863	Greek
4865	Roman (Tesserae)
4867.A-Z	Other (not A-Z)
	Medieval and modern
4871	General works
4873	Medieval
4877	Renaissance
	Modern
4881	General works
4883	16th-17th centuries
4885	18th century
4887	19th century
4889	20th century
	By region or country
4901-4910	United States (Table C11 modified)
	By period
4905	Colonial
4906	Early national
4911-4920	Canada (Table C11)
4921-4925	Mexico (Table C12)
4926-4929	Central America (Table C12a)
4930	Belize
4931-4935	Costa Rica (Table C12)
4936-4940	Guatemala (Table C12)
4941-4945	Honduras (Table C12)

Tokens
  By region or country
    Central America -- Continued

4946-4950	Nicaragua (Table C12)
4951-4955	Panama (Table C12)
4956-4960	El Salvador (Table C12)
4961-4964	West Indies (Table C12a)
4966	Bahamas
4967-4971	Cuba (Table C12)
4972	Haiti
4973	Dominican Republic
4975-4979	Jamaica (Table C12)
4980-4984	Puerto Rico (Table C12)
4985.A-Z	Other West Indian islands, A-Z
4986-4989	South America (Table C12a)
4991-4995	Argentina (Table C12)
4996-5000	Bolivia (Table C12)
5001-5005	Brazil (Table C12)
5006-5010	Chile (Table C12)
5011-5015	Colombia (Table C12)
5016-5020	Ecuador (Table C12)
5021	French Guiana
5022	Guyana
5026-5030	Paraguay (Table C12)
5031-5035	Peru (Table C12)
5035.5	Suriname
5036-5040	Uruguay (Table C12)
5041-5045	Venezuela (Table C12)
5046-5049	Europe (Table C12a)
	Great Britain. England
5051	Periodicals. Societies. Serials
5052	Catalogs
5053	General works
5054	General special
	By period
5055	Medieval
5056	16th-18th centuries
5057	19th-20th centuries
5058.A-Z	Local, A-Z
5058.4	Northern Ireland
5058.6	Scotland
5060	Ireland
5061-5070	Austria (Table C11)
5071-5080	France (Table C11)
5081-5085	Germany (Table C12)
	Including West Germany
5086-5090	East Germany (Table C12)

	Tokens
	By region or country
	Europe -- Continued
5091-5095	Greece (Table C12)
5096-5105	Italy (Table C11)
5111-5115	Belgium (Table C12)
5116-5120	Netherlands (Table C12)
5121-5125	Russia (Table C12)
5127	Poland
	Scandinavia
5129	General works
5130-5134	Denmark (Table C12)
5135	Iceland
5136-5140	Norway (Table C12)
5141-5145	Sweden (Table C12)
5146-5150	Spain (Table C12)
5151-5155	Portugal (Table C12)
5156-5160	Switzerland (Table C12)
	Balkan States
5166	Albania
5168-5172	Bulgaria (Table C12)
5175-5179	Romania (Table C12)
5180-5184	Yugoslavia (Table C12)
5185.A-Z	Other European countries, A-Z
5186-5189	Asia (Table C12a)
5191-5195	China (Table C12)
5196-5200	Indonesia (Table C12)
5201-5205	India (Table C12)
5206-5210	Sri Lanka (Table C12)
5211-5215	Thailand (Table C12)
5216-5220	Japan (Table C12)
5221-5225	Iran (Table C12)
5226-5230	Philippines (Table C12)
5231-5235	Korea (Table C12)
5236-5240	Turkey (Table C12)
5243.A-Z	Other divisions of Asia, A-Z
5246-5249	Africa (Table C12a)
5251-5255	Egypt (Table C12)
5256-5260	South Africa (Table C12)
5261-5265	Algeria (Table C12)
5266-5270	Tanzania (Table C12)
5271-5275	Mozambique (Table C12)
5278.A-Z	Other divisions of Africa, A-Z
5281-5285	Australia (Table C12)
5326-5330	New Zealand (Table C12)
5336.A-Z	Pacific islands, A-Z
	For Hawaiian Islands, see CJ4909.H3

	Tokens -- Continued
	Special uses of tokens
5350	Commercial, industrial, etc.
	For printers' tokens see Z234
	Religious
5400	General works
	Communion tokens
5407	General works
5413.A-Z	By denomination, A-Z
5413.P8	Presbyterian
5415.A-Z	By region or country, A-Z
	For special denominations see CJ5413.A+
5450	Jetons, counters, méreaux, etc.
	Medals and medallions
	For military medals see UB430+
	For naval medals see VB330+
5501	Periodicals. Societies. Serials
5502	Congresses
	Collected works (nonserial)
5505	Several authors
5506	Individual authors
	Exhibitions
5507	International. By date
5508.A-Z	Other. By place, A-Z
	Museums. Collections
	Public
5509	General works
5510.A-Z	By region or country, A-Z

Under each country:

.x	General works
.x2A-.x2Z	Special. By city, A-Z

	Private
5511	General works
5512.A-Z	By region or country, A-Z

Under each country:

.x	General works
.x2A-.x2Z	By collector, A-Z

	Sales catalogs
5513	Auction
5514	Dealers'
	Philosophy. Theory
5517	General works
5519	Relation to art
5521	Relation to history
5525	Study and teaching
5535	Dictionaries. Encyclopedias
	General works

	Medals and medallions	
	General works -- Continued	
5538	Through 1800	
5539	1801-	
5543	Handbooks, manuals, etc.	
5549	General special	
	Execution. Technique	
5555	General works	
5557	Types	
5569	Iconography	
	Ancient	
5581	Periodicals. Societies. Serials	
	Collected works (nonserial)	
5583	Several authors	
5584	Individual authors	
5585	Exhibitions	
	Museums. Collections	
	Public	
5587	General works	
5588.A-Z	By region or country, A-Z	
	Under each country:	
	.x	*General works*
	.x2A-.x2Z	*Special. By city, A-Z*
	Private	
5589	General works	
5590.A-Z	By region or country, A-Z	
	Under each country:	
	.x	*General works*
	.x2A-.x2Z	*By collector, A-Z*
5591	Sales catalogs	
	General works	
5595	Through 1800	
5597	1801-	
5598	Handbooks, manuals, etc.	
5605	General special	
5615	Iconography	
5625	Greek	
	Roman	
5641	Periodicals. Societies. Serials	
	Collected works (nonserial)	
5643	Several authors	
5644	Individual authors	
5645	Exhibitions	
	Museums. Collections	
	Public	
5647	General works	

Medals and medallions
  Ancient
  Roman
  Museums. Collections
  Public -- Continued
5648.A-Z   By region or country, A-Z
                  Under each country:
                  .x   *General works*
                  .x2A-.x2Z   *Special. By city, A-Z*
                Private
5649   General works
5650.A-Z   By region or country, A-Z
                  Under each country:
                  .x   *General works*
                  .x2A-.x2Z   *By collector, A-Z*
5651   Sales catalogs
5655   General works
5660   Handbooks, manuals, etc.
5665   General special
5675   Iconography
5681.A-Z   Persons, A-Z
5683.A-Z   Events, A-Z
5685.A-Z   Local, A-Z
5690.A-Z   Other, A-Z
              Medieval and modern
                Periodicals, societies, serials, etc.
                  see CJ5501+
                General works
5723   Through 1800
5725   1801-
5727   Handbooks, manuals, etc.
5733   General special
5737   Execution. Technique
5751   Iconography
                By period
                  Medieval
5761   General works
5763   General special
                      Including crusades
                  Renaissance
5767   General works
5769   Early
5770   High
5771   Later
                  Modern
5775   General works
5777   16th-17th centuries

	Medals and medallions
	Medieval and modern
	By period
	Modern -- Continued
5778	18th century
5779	19th century
5780	20th century
5793.A-Z	Special subjects, A-Z
	For works on medals issued by a specific society, see the society in classes A-Z
5793.A3	Aeronautics
5793.A4	America
5793.A72	Architecture
5793.A8	Automobiles
5793.B68	Boy Scouts
5793.F67	Forests and forestry
5793.H92	Huguenots
5793.L3	Labor
5793.L5	Lifesaving
5793.L7	Longevity
5793.M4	Medicine
5793.M55	Mineral industries
5793.P4	Peace
5793.P53	Pharmacy
5793.P66	Popes
	Printing (Medallic history) see Z234
5793.R2	Railways (Commemorative medals)
5793.R34	Religion
	Cf. BX2310.M5 Use of devotional medals in the Catholic Church
5793.S5	Shooting
5793.S6	Sports
5793.W65	Women
	By region or country
	For works limited to the ancient period of a region or country see CJ5581+
	For works on medals relating to a special subject see CJ5793.A+
5795	America (General)
5801-5819	United States (Table C13 modified)
	By period
(5810)	Medieval
	This number not valid for the United States
5811	Colonial
5812	Early national
5821-5829	Canada (Table C14)
	Latin America (General)

Medals and medallions
  By region or country
    Latin America (General) -- Continued

5830	General works
5831-5839	Mexico (Table C14)
5841-5845	Central America (Table C15 modified)
(5845.A-Z)	Local, A-Z
	see CJ5846+
5846-5850	Belize (Table C15)
5851-5855	Costa Rica (Table C15)
5861-5865	Guatemala (Table C15)
5871-5875	Honduras (Table C15)
5881-5885	Nicaragua (Table C15)
5891-5895	Panama (Table C15)
5901-5905	El Salvador (Table C15)
5911-5915	West Indies (Table C15 modified)
(5915.A-Z)	Local, A-Z
	see CJ5916+
5916-5920	Bahamas (Table C15)
5921-5925	Cuba (Table C15)
5931-5935	Haiti (Table C15)
5941-5945	Dominican Republic (Table C15)
5951-5955	Jamaica (Table C15)
5961-5965	Puerto Rico (Table C15)
5968.A-Z	Other West Indian islands, A-Z
5971-5978	South America (Table C14a)
5981-5989	Argentina (Table C14)
5991-5999	Bolivia (Table C14)
6001-6009	Brazil (Table C14)
6011-6019	Chile (Table C14)
6021-6029	Colombia (Table C14)
6031-6039	Ecuador (Table C14)
6041-6049	Guyana (Table C14)
6051-6059	Paraguay (Table C14)
6061-6069	Peru (Table C14)
6071-6079	Uruguay (Table C14)
6081-6089	Venezuela (Table C14)
6090.A-Z	Other South American countries, A-Z
6091-6098	Europe (Table 14 nos. 0-7)
	Great Britain. England
6101	Periodicals. Societies. Serials
	Museums
	Public
6102	General works
6102.2.A-Z	By city, A-Z
	Private
6103	General works

CJ

Medals and medallions
By region or country
Europe
Great Britain. England
Museums
Private -- Continued
6103.3.A-Z   By collector, A-Z
6104   Sales catalogs
6105   General works
6106   General special
For works on medals relating to a special subject, see
CJ5793
Biography of medalists
6108   Collective
6109.A-Z   Individual artists, A-Z
By period
6110   Medieval
6111   Renaissance, 15th-17th centuries
6112   18th century
6113   19th-20th centuries
6115.A-Z   Persons and families, A-Z
Class here medals of individuals and families in all fields
6115.5.A-Z   Events, A-Z
6117.A-Z   Local, A-Z
6117.5   Northern Ireland
6118   Wales
6119   Scotland
6120   Ireland
6121-6139   Austria (Table C13)
6140   Czechoslovakia. Czech Republic
6140.5   Slovakia
6141-6159   France (Table C13)
6161-6169   Germany (Table C13)
Including West Germany
6180   East Germany
6181-6189   Greece (Table C14)
6190   Hungary
6191-6209   Italy (Table C13)
6211-6218   Low countries (Table C14a)
6219   Luxembourg
6221-6229   Belgium (Table C14)
6231-6239   Netherlands (Table C14)
6241-6249   Russia (Table C14)
6250   Poland
6251-6259   Scandinavia (Table C14a)
6261-6269   Denmark (Table C14)
6270   Finland

Medals and medallions
By region or country
Europe
Scandinavia -- Continued

6271	Iceland
6281-6289	Norway (Table C14)
6291-6299	Sweden (Table C14)
6301-6309	Spain (Table C14)
6311-6319	Portugal (Table C14)
6321-6329	Switzerland (Table C14)
	Balkan States
6331-6335	Albania (Table C14)
6335.5	Bosnia and Hercegovina
6336-6344	Bulgaria (Table C14)
6345-6349	Croatia (Table C15)
6350	Macedonia (Republic)
6351-6359	Romania (Table C14)
6360	Slovenia
6361-6369	Yugoslavia (Table C14)
6380.A-Z	Other European countries, A-Z
6381-6388	Asia (Table C14a)
6391-6399	China (Table C14)
6401-6409	Indonesia (Table C14)
6411-6419	India (Table C14)
6421-6429	Sri Lanka (Table C14)
6431-6435	Thailand (Table C15)
6441-6449	Japan (Table C14)
6451-6459	Iran (Table C14)
6461-6469	Philippines (Table C14)
6471-6479	Turkey (Table C14)
6485.A-Z	Other Asian countries, A-Z
6491-6498	Africa (Table C14a)
6501-6509	Egypt (Table C14)
6511-6519	South Africa (Table C14)
6521-6525	Algeria (Table C15)
6526-6530	Madagascar (Table C15)
6531-6535	Tanzania (Table C15)
6536-6540	Mozambique (Table C15)
6559.A-Z	Other African countries, A-Z
6561-6569	Australia (Table C14)
6651-6659	New Zealand (Table C14)
6661.A-Z	Pacific islands, A-Z
	For Hawaiian Islands, see CJ5818.H3

Inscriptions. Epigraphy
   Including archaeological reports
   For philological studies of inscriptions, see classes P - PT
   Cf. CD5001+ Seals
   Cf. CJ71 Numismatics
   Cf. E98.P34 Petroglyphs (North American Indians)
   Cf. GN799.P4 Petroglyphs
   Cf. GT3912+ Graffiti
   Cf. P211+ History of writing
   Cf. PJ1091+ Egyptian hieroglyphics
   Cf. PJ3191+ Cuneiform writing
   Cf. PN6288.5+ Epitaphs

1	Periodicals. Societies. Serials
15	Congresses
	Collected works (nonserial)
20	Several authors
20.5	Individual authors
25.A-Z	Museums, libraries, and other institutions. By place, A-Z
	For inscriptions in special languages, see CN355; CN515; etc.
25.N3	Naples. Museo nazionale
25.R7	Rome. Museo capitolino
30.A-Z	Private collections. By collector, A-Z
	For inscriptions in special languages, see CN355; CN515; etc.
	Philosophy. Theory
40	General works
41	Relation to archaeology, history, etc.
	Relation to architectural decoration see NA4050.I5
42	Relation to religion
	Methodology. Technique
44	General works
46	Photographic methods
50	Study and teaching
55	History of epigraphy (General)
	For the history of epigraphy in particular languages, see the language, e.g. Egyptian PJ1051+
	Biography of epigraphists
	For epigraphists specializing in special languages, see the language, e.g., Egyptian PJ1063+
61	Collective
62.A-Z	Individual, A-Z
	Champollion see PJ1064.C6
70	Dictionaries. Encyclopedias
	General works
74	Early works through 1800
75	1801-
77	General special
86	Juvenile works

90	Addresses, essays, lectures
99	Forgeries of inscriptions
110	Collections of inscriptions (Books)
	Including miscellaneous selections
	By period
	Ancient inscriptions
120	General works
	Ancient Oriental, Asian, or African languages (General)
	For inscriptions in special languages, see subclasses PJ - PL.
	For hieroglyphics, cuneiform inscriptions, etc., see subclass PJ
130	General works
135	Classic Orient (General)
	Chinese see PL2447+
	Egyptian
	see PJ1521+ PJ1670; PJ2193; etc.
	Hamitic see PJ991+
	Hittite see P945.A1+
	Sanskrit
	see PK2976; etc.
	Semitic
	see PJ3081+ PJ3191+ etc.
	Classical languages
	Including Greek, Latin, Etruscan, etc.
339.2	Museums, libraries, and other institutions
	see CN25; CN355; CN515; etc.
340	General works
341.2	By region or country
	see the language of the inscription, including CN380+
	Greek; for two or more languages, unless one strongly predominates, see CN900+
	Greek
350	General works
355.A-Z	Museums, libraries, and other institutions. By place, A-Z
360	Collections of inscriptions (Books)
360.C6	Corpus inscriptionum graecarum
360.I6	Inscriptiones graecae
362	Inscriptions in Greek dialects
	Inscriptions by subject
	Historical records
365	General works
367.A-Z	Special, A-Z
	Monumentum ancyranum see DG279
	Paros, Chronicle of (Marmor Parium) see DF12.P3; PA4263.P2
368	Magic

CN

	By period
	Ancient inscriptions
	Classical languages
	Greek
	Inscriptions by subject -- Continued
370	Political and social
373	Religious
	Cf. CN750+ Early Christian inscriptions
375.A-Z	Other special, A-Z
375.A2	Abbreviations
375.A7	Artists' signatures
375.D4	Defixionum tabellae
375.E6	Epitaphs and sepulchral inscriptions (General)
	For local see CN379.2+
	Cf. PN6288.5+ Epitaphs
375.H6	Honorifics
375.V3	Vase inscriptions
375.V4	Verse inscriptions
375.V6	Votive offerings
	By region or country
	Greece
	General works see CN350
380.A-Z	By region, A-Z
	e.g.
380.A7	Argolis
380.D4	Delos
	By city
384	Athens
385.A-Z	Other cities, A-Z
	e.g.
385.M3	Magnesia
	Italy
390	General works
393.A-Z	By region, A-Z
	e.g.
393.M3	Magna Graecia
393.S3	Sicily
	By city
395	Rome
397.A-Z	Other cities, A-Z
	e.g.
397.H4	Heraclea
398.A-Z	Other European countries, A-Z
	e.g.
398.R9	Russia
400	Asia. The Orient
405	Near East

	By period
	Ancient inscriptions
	Classical languages
	Greek
	By region or country -- Continued
	Asia Minor. Turkey
410	General works
415.A-Z	By city, etc., A-Z
	e.g.
415.I7	Ionia
415.L8	Lycia
415.M8	Mysia
415.P4	Phrygia
415.T7	Troy
420	Crete
	For Minoan see P1035+
430	Cyprus
	Egypt
440	General works
441.A-Z	Local, A-Z
	e.g.
441.A2	Abydos
450.A-Z	Other local, A-Z
	e.g.
450.S5	Sinai
455	Byzantine
	Ancient languages and dialects of Italy
	Cf. PA2391+ Philology
460	General works
	Illyrian
470	General works
	Messapian. Iapygian
472	General works
473	Venetic
475	Ligurian
477	Celtic (Gaulish)
	Cf. GN825 Gaulish (General)
479	Etruscan
	Italic dialects
	Cf. PA2420+ Latin philology
480	General works
	Special
	Osco-Umbrian
483	General works
484	Oscan
	Umbrian
485	General works

CN

By period
Ancient inscriptions
Classical languages
Ancient languages and dialects of Italy
Italic dialects
Special
Osco-Umbrian
Umbrian -- Continued
Tabulae Iguvinae see PA2461
Sabellian

487	General works
488	Aequian
489	Marrucinian
490	Marsian
491	Paelignian
492	Sabine
493	Vestinian
494	Volscian
495	Latin-Faliscan
496	Faliscan
496.5	Picenian inscriptions
498	Praenestian
498.5	Raetian
499	Sicel

Latin

510	General works
513	General special
515.A-Z	Museums, libraries, and other institutions. By place, A-Z
520	Collections of inscriptions (Books)
	e.g.
520.C6	Corpus inscriptionum latinarum
521	Selections

Inscriptions. By subject
For inscriptions of particular places on particular subjects see CN530+

523	Religious
	Cf. CN750+ Early Christian inscriptions
525	Political and social
527	Historical records
	Cf. PA6220.A85 Augustus, emperor of Rome (Latin literature)
528.A-Z	Other special, A-Z
528.A7	Artists' signatures
528.A8	Autobiographical elements
528.D4	Defixionum tabellae

By period
  Ancient inscriptions
    Classical languages
      Latin
        Inscriptions. By subject
          Other special, A-Z -- Continued

528.E6	Epitaphs and sepulchral inscriptions (General)
	For local see CN530+
	Cf. PN6288.5+ Epitaphs
528.M6	Military inscriptions
528.V4	Verse inscriptions
529.A-Z	Inscriptions on special articles, A-Z
	Bricks see CN529.T5
529.M5	Milestones
529.S7	Stele
529.S94	Swords
529.T5	Tiles and bricks
	Tombs see CN528.E6
529.V3	Vases
529.5.A-Z	Special inscriptions. By name, A-Z
	For named inscriptions on special articles see CN528.A+
	For special types of named inscriptions see CN529.A+
529.5.D8	Duenos inscriptions
	By region or country
	Europe
	Italy
	Class here only those inscriptions that are expressly of Italian origin. For Roman inscriptions in general, see CN510+
530	General works
532.A-Z	By region or kingdom, etc. A-Z
	e.g.
532.B6	Bologna (Province)
532.C7	Cremona (Province)
532.M3	Magna Graecia
532.N3	Naples (Kingdom)
532.S5	Sicily
	By city
533	Pompeii
535	Rome
537.A-Z	Other cities, A-Z
	Other European countries
	Austria
540	General works
543.A-Z	Local, A-Z

By period
 Ancient inscriptions
  Classical languages
   Latin
    By region or country
     Europe
      Other European countries -- Continued

550	Belgium
560	Czechoslovakia
565	Finland
	France
570	General works
573.A-Z	Local, A-Z
	e.g.
573.B3	Basque Provinces
573.C6	Côte d'Or
573.G3	Gascony
573.M6	Moselle
575	Gaul (Ancient)
	Germany
580	General works
	Including West Germany
583.A-Z	By region or state, A-Z
585.A-Z	Local, A-Z
	East Germany
587	General works
588.A-Z	Local, A-Z
	Great Britain. England
	Cf. DA145+ Roman antiquities
590	General works
593.A-C593.Z	England. By county, A-Z
595.A-C595.Z	England. By city or other local, A-Z
597	Northern Ireland
599	Scotland
601	Wales
605.A-Z	Other special, A-Z
605.C4	Channel Islands
610	Greece
615	Hungary
	Ireland
617	General works
618.A-Z	Local, A-Z
620	Netherlands
625	Poland
	Portugal
630	General works
631.A-Z	Local, A-Z

	By period
	Ancient inscriptions
	Classical languages
	Latin
	By region or country
	Europe
	Other European countries -- Continued
635	Romania
640	Russia
	Scandinavia
645	General works
650	Denmark
655	Norway
660	Sweden
	Spain
670	General works
675.A-Z	Local, A-Z
680	Switzerland
690	Yugoslavia
695.A-Z	Other European countries, A-Z
	Asia
700	General works
702	Near East
703	Asia Minor. Turkey
705.A-Z	Other regions or countries, A-Z
	Africa
710	General works
715	North Africa
720	Algeria
725	Egypt
730.A-Z	Other countries, A-Z
	Medieval Latin
	see CN510+
740	Modern Latin
	Celtiberian see P1081
	Celtic see CN477; CN815+
	Runic see PD2001+
745	Jewish inscriptions (General)
	Including inscriptions in Greek or Latin; for inscriptions in other languages, see the language, e.g. PJ5034.4+ Hebrew
	Early Christian inscriptions
	Including early Christian inscriptions in Latin; for inscriptions in other languages, see the language, including CN350+
	Greek
750	General works
753.A-Z	By country, A-Z
753.E3	Egypt

	By region or country
	United States -- Continued
870	General works
871.A-Z	By region, state, etc., A-Z
872.A-Z	By city, A-Z
	Canada
873	General works
874.A-Z	By region, province, etc., A-Z
875.A-Z	By city, A-Z
	Mexico
876	General works
877.A-Z	By region, state, etc., A-Z
878.A-Z	By city, A-Z
	Central America
	For Indian inscriptions, see class F
882	General works
884	Costa Rica
	South America
	For Indian inscriptions, see class F
886	General works
888	Brazil
	Europe
900	General works
	Austria
910	General works
913.A-Z	By region, province, etc., A-Z
915.A-Z	By city, A-Z
920	Balkan States (General)
	Belgium
925	General works
926.A-Z	Local, A-Z
	Bulgaria
930	General works
931.A-Z	Local, A-Z
	Czechoslovakia
935	General works
936.A-Z	Local, A-Z
	Denmark see CN1075+
	Finland
940	General works
941.A-Z	Local, A-Z
	France
945	General works
946.A-Z	By region, province, etc., A-Z
946.C4	Charente Inférieure
946.G2	Gascony
	By city

	By region or country
	Europe
	France
	By city -- Continued
947	Paris
948.A-Z	Other cities, A-Z
	Germany
	Including West Germany
950	General works
953.A-Z	By region, state, etc., A-Z
953.R4	Rhine Province
955.A-Z	By city, A-Z
	East Germany
956	General works
957.A-Z	Local, A-Z
	Great Britain
960	General works
963.A-Z	England. By region, county, etc., A-Z
965.A-Z	England. By city, town, etc., A-Z
	Northern Ireland
970	General works
973.A-Z	By region, county, etc., A-Z
975.A-Z	By city, town, A-Z
	Scotland
980	General works
983.A-Z	By region, county, etc., A-Z
985.A-Z	By city, town, A-Z
	Wales
990	General works
993.A-Z	By region, county, etc., A-Z
995.A-Z	By city, town, A-Z
997.A-Z	Other special (Islands, etc.), A-Z
	Greece
1000	General works
	Ancient Greek inscriptions see CN350+
1003.A-Z	By region, island, etc., A-Z
	e.g.
1003.C7	Crete
1003.M3	Macedonia
1005.A-Z	By city, A-Z
	Hungary
1006	General works
1007.A-Z	Local, A-Z
	Iceland see CN1077+
	Ireland
1008	General works
1009.A-Z	Local, A-Z

	By region or country
	Europe -- Continued
	Italy
1010	General works
	Ancient and Medieval Latin inscriptions
	see CN510+
1013.A-Z	By region, province, etc., A-Z
	e.g.
1013.F7	Friuli-Venezia Giulia
1013.L5	Liguria
1013.S5	Sicily
1015.A-Z	By city, A-Z
	e.g.
1015.R6	Rome
	Netherlands
1020	General works
1021.A-Z	Local, A-Z
	Norway see CN1080+
	Poland
1030	General works
1031.A-Z	Local, A-Z
	Portugal
1040	General works
1041.A-Z	Local, A-Z
	Romania
1050	General works
1051.A-Z	Local, A-Z
	Russia. Former Russian republics
1060	General works
1063.A-Z	By region, province, etc., A-Z
1065.A-Z	By city, A-Z
	Scandinavia
	Cf. PD2001+ Runes
1070	General works
	Denmark
1075	General works
1076.A-Z	Local, A-Z
	Iceland
1077	General works
1078.A-Z	Local, A-Z
	Norway
1080	General works
1081.A-Z	Local, A-Z
	Sweden
1085	General works
1086.A-Z	Local, A-Z
	Spain

CN

	By region or country
	Asia
	Korea -- Continued
1183.A-Z	Local, A-Z
	Syria
1190	General works
1191.A-Z	Local, A-Z
	Israel
1193	General works
1194.A-Z	Local, A-Z
	Iran
1200	General works
1201.A-Z	Local, A-Z
	Philippines
1210	General works
1211.A-Z	Local, A-Z
	Burma. Myanmar
1213	General works
1214.A-Z	Local, A-Z
	Thailand
1220	General works
1221.A-Z	Local, A-Z
1230.A-Z	Other, A-Z
1230.C3	Cambodia
1230.C4	Ceylon. Sri Lanka
1230.I8	Iraq
	Sri Lanka see CN1230.C4
1230.V53	Vietnam
	Africa
1300	General works
1305	North Africa (General)
1307	South Africa
	Egypt
	For ancient Egyptian inscriptions, see PJ1521+ PJ1670; etc.
	For coptic inscriptions see PJ2193
1310	General works
1311.A-Z	Local, A-Z
1320.A-Z	Other regions or countries, A-Z
	e.g.
1320.A4	Algeria
1320.E8	Ethiopia
	Australia
1340	General works
1345.A-Z	Local, A-Z
1347	New Zealand
	Oceania
1350	General works

CN

By region or country
Oceania -- Continued
1355.A-Z Individual islands, A-Z
For Easter Island see F3169

	Heraldry
	For heraldry combined with genealogy see CS1+
1	Periodicals. Societies. Serials
2	Congresses
	Collected works (nonserial)
4	Several authors
5	Individual authors
9	Museums. Exhibitions
	Subarrange by city or other place of exhibition
11	Directories
13	Dictionaries. Encyclopedias
	Philosophy. Theory. Relation to other topics
14	General works
15	Relation to art, architecture, etc.
16	Relation to literature (General)
	For heraldry in the writings of a particular literary author, see the author, e.g. PR3069.H4 Shakespeare
	Relation to seals see CD5037
	History see CR151+
	General works
19	Through 1800
21	1801-
28	General special
41.A-Z	Special branches, charges, etc., A-Z
41.C3	Cadency
41.C4	Canting arms
41.C5	Collar
41.C7	Crosses
41.F4	Fishes
41.F6	Flowers (Fleur-de-lis, rose, etc.)
	Crests, monograms, devices, badges, mottoes, etc.
	Cf. NK1585 Emblems
51	General works
53	General special
	Including heraldic aspects of regalia, crown jewels, etc.
	Cf. CR4480 Insignia of royalty and nobility
	Cf. NK7400+ Decorative arts
	Crests
55	General works
57.A-Z	By region or country, A-Z
	Monograms
61	General works
62.A-Z	By region or country, A-Z
	Devices and badges
67	General works
69.A-Z	By region or country, A-Z
	Mottoes

CR

Crests, monograms, devices, badges, mottoes, etc.
    Mottoes -- Continued

73	General works
75.A-Z	By region or country, A-Z
79	Battles cries. War cries

Shields and supporters

91	General works
93.A-Z	By region or country, A-Z

Flags, banners, and standards
        Cf. CR191+ Public and official heraldry
        Cf. JC345+ Political theory
        Cf. UC590+ Military standards

101	General works
	For flag-waving exercises see GV488
102	Conservation and restoration

By period

105	Early
107	Medieval
109	Modern
112	International or World flag
112.5	Spanish-American flag

By region or country
    United States

113	General works
113.2	States (Collectively)
113.5	Confederacy
113.7	New England
114.A-.W	By state, A-W
114.5.A-Z	By city, A-Z
115.A-Z	Other regions or countries, A-Z

       Under each country:

.x	*General works*
.x15A-.x15Z	*By region, province, state, etc., A-Z*
.x2A-.x2Z	*By city, A-Z*

Printers' marks see Z235+
Armorial bookbindings see Z266+
Armorial bookplates see Z993+
Armorial china see NK4374

History

151	General works
153	Early works
155	Ancient

Medieval

157	General works
158	Muslim. Saracen
159	Modern
	By region or country see CR1190+

	Law, grants of arms, etc. Patents. Regulation
165	General works
167.A-Z	By region or country, A-Z
	Right to bear arms
171	General works
175	Mutation. Alteration
179	Use and abuses. Usurpation
	Kings-at-arms, heralds (Heralds' college)
183	General works
185.A-Z	By region or country, A-Z
	Public and official heraldry
	Including general albums on national arms, emblems, flags, flowers, seals, songs, etc.
	Cf. CR101+ Flags, banners, and standards
	Cf. JC345+ Political theory
191	General works
	By region or country
	North America
199	General works
200-209	United States (Table C16)
210-219	Canada (Table C16)
220-229	Mexico (Table C16)
	Central America
230	General works
235-239	Belize (Table C17)
240-244	Costa Rica (Table C17)
250-254	Guatemala (Table C17)
260-264	Honduras (Table C17)
270-274	Nicaragua (Table C17)
280-284	Panama (Table C17)
290-294	El Salvador (Table C17)
	West Indies
304	General works
305-309	Bahamas (Table C17)
310-314	Cuba (Table C17)
320-324	Haiti (Table C17)
325-329	Dominican Republic (Table C17)
330-334	Jamaica (Table C17)
340-344	Puerto Rico (Table C17)
350.A-Z	Other West Indian islands, A-Z
	South America
369	General works
370-379	Argentina (Table C16)
380-389	Bolivia (Table C16)
390-399	Brazil (Table C16)
400-409	Chile (Table C16)
410-419	Colombia (Table C16)

CR

Public and official heraldry
By region or country
South America -- Continued

420-429	Ecuador (Table C16)
430-434	French Guiana (Table C17)
435-439	Guyana (Table C17)
440-449	Paraguay (Table C16)
450-454	Peru (Table C17)
455-459	Suriname (Table C17)
460-469	Uruguay (Table C16)
470-479	Venezuela (Table C16)
479.5.A-Z	South Atlantic islands, A-Z
	Europe
489	General works
489.5	Eastern Europe (General)
490-499	Great Britain. England (Table C16)
500-509	Wales (Table C16)
510-519	Scotland (Table C16)
520-524	Northern Ireland (Table C17)
525-529	Ireland (Table C17)
530-539	Austria (Table C16)
539.5	Hungary
540-549	France (Table C16)
550-559	Germany (Table C16)
	Including West Germany
559.2	East Germany
560-569	Greece (Table C16)
570-579	Italy (Table C16)
579.5	Malta
590-599	Belgium (Table C16)
600-609	Netherlands (Table C16)
(609.5)	Eastern Europe
	see CR489.5
610-614	Russia. Former Soviet republics (Table C17)
614.2	Belarus
614.3	Moldova
614.4	Ukraine
615-619	Poland (Table C17)
	Baltic States
619.2	General works
619.3	Latvia
619.4	Lithuania
619.5	Estonia
620-624	Czechoslovakia. Czech Republic (Table C17)
624.5	Slovakia
	Scandinavia
629	General works

CR

	Ecclesiastical and sacred heraldry -- Continued
1115	Popes and cardinals
	Episcopal
1119	General works
1121.A-Z	By region or country, A-Z
	Religious orders
1127	General works
1129.A-Z	By order, A-Z
1131.A-Z	By region or country, A-Z
	Family heraldry
1179	General collections, rolls, etc.
1187.A-Z	Particular families or individuals, covering more than one country, A-Z
	By region or country
1190-1199	North America (Table C19a)
1200-1219	United States (Table C18)
1230-1249	Canada (Table C18)
1260-1269	Mexico (Table C19)
1280-1289	Central America (Table C19a)
1290-1299	Belize (Table C19)
1300-1309	Costa Rica (Table C19)
1310-1319	Guatemala (Table C19)
1320-1329	Honduras (Table C19)
1330-1339	Nicaragua (Table C19)
1340-1349	Panama (Table C19)
1350-1359	El Salvador (Table C19)
1360-1369	West Indies (Table C19a)
1370-1379	Bahamas (Table C19)
1380-1389	Cuba (Table C19)
1390-1399	Haiti (Table C19)
1400-1409	Jamaica (Table C19)
1410-1419	Puerto Rico (Table C19)
1425.A-Z	Other West Indian islands, A-Z
1440-1449	South America (Table C19a)
1450-1459	Argentina (Table C19)
1460-1469	Bolivia (Table C19)
1470-1479	Brazil (Table C19)
1480-1489	Chile (Table C19)
1490-1499	Colombia (Table C19)
1500-1509	Ecuador (Table C19)
1510-1519	French Guiana (Table C19)
1520-1529	Guyana (Table C19)
1530-1539	Paraguay (Table C19)
1540-1549	Peru (Table C19)
1549.5	Suriname
1550-1559	Uruguay (Table C19)
1560-1569	Venezuela (Table C19)

Family heraldry
By region or country -- Continued

1600-1609	Europe (Table C19a)
1610-1629	Great Britain. England (Table C18)
1640-1649	Wales (Table C19)
1650-1669	Scotland (Table C18)
1670-1679	Northern Ireland (Table C19)
1680-1699	Ireland (Table C18)
1700-1719	Austria (Table C18)
1720-1729	Czechoslovakia. Czech Republic (Table C19)
1730-1739	Slovakia (Table C19)
1770-1779	Hungary (Table C19)
1790-1809	France (Table C18)
1820-1839	Germany (Table C18)
	Including West Germany
1840-1859	East Germany (Table C18)
1940-1959	Greece (Table C18)
1960-1979	Italy (Table C18)
2000-2009	Belgium (Table C19)
2010-2019	Netherlands (Table C19)
2020-2029	Luxembourg (Table C19)
2030-2049	Russia. Former Soviet republics (Table C18)
2060-2069	Poland (Table C19)
2080-2089	Lithuania (Table C19)
	Scandinavia
2090	General works
2100-2109	Denmark (Table C19)
2110-2119	Norway (Table C19)
2120-2129	Sweden (Table C19)
2130-2139	Finland (Table C19)
2140-2159	Spain (Table C18)
2160-2169	Portugal (Table C19)
2180-2189	Switzerland (Table C19)
	Balkan States
2210-2219	Albania (Table C19)
2220-2229	Bulgaria (Table C19)
2240-2249	Romania (Table C19)
2250-2259	Yugoslavia (Table C19)
2280-2289	Asia (Table C19a)
2300-2309	Afghanistan (Table C19)
2320-2329	Saudi Arabia (Table C19)
2340-2349	Pakistan (Table C19)
2360-2369	China (Table C19)
2380-2389	Indonesia (Table C19)
2430-2439	India (Table C19)
2440-2449	Sri Lanka (Table C19)
2490-2499	Thailand (Table C19)

CR

	Family heraldry
	By region or country
	Asia -- Continued
2520-2529	Malaysia (Table C19)
2550-2559	Japan (Table C19)
2570-2579	Korea (Table C19)
2610-2619	Philippines (Table C19)
2620-2629	Iran (Table C19)
2670-2679	Turkey (Table C19)
2700-2709	Israel (Table C19)
2710-2719	Syria (Table C19)
2735.A-Z	Other Asian countries, A-Z
2750-2759	Africa (Table C19a)
2770-2779	Ethiopia (Table C19)
2790-2799	South Africa (Table C19)
2840-2849	Zaire (Table C19)
2850-2859	Egypt (Table C19)
2880-2889	Algeria (Table C19)
2890-2899	Madagascar (Table C19)
2900-2909	Tanzania (Table C19)
2920-2929	Liberia (Table C19)
2940-2949	Morocco (Table C19)
2960-2969	Mozambique (Table C19)
3000.A-Z	Other African countries, A-Z
3200-3219	Australia (Table C18)
3240-3259	New Zealand (Table C18)
	Pacific islands
3380	General works
3395.A-Z	Local, A-Z
	Hawaiian Islands, see CR1217
	Titles of honor, rank, precedence, etc.
	General works
	Through 1800
3499	Latin
3501	English
3503	French
3505	German
3507	Italian
3509	Spanish
3511	Other (not A-Z)
	1801-
3514	Latin
3515	English
3517	French
3519	German
3521	Italian
3523	Spanish

	Titles of honor, rank, precedence, etc.
	General works
	1801- -- Continued
3525.A-Z	Other (not A-Z)
3535	General special
	Order of precedence
3575	General works
	By region or country see CR3599+
	By race
3585	Jews
	By region or country
	North America
3599	General works
3600-3609	United States (Table C20)
3610-3619	Canada (Table C20)
3620-3629	Mexico (Table C20)
	Central America
3630	General works
3635	Belize
3640	Costa Rica
3650	Guatemala
3660	Honduras
3670	Nicaragua
3680	Panama
3690	El Salvador
	West Indies
3700	General works
3705	Bahamas
3710	Cuba
3720	Haiti
3725	Dominican Republic
3730	Jamaica
3740	Puerto Rico
3750.A-Z	Other West Indian islands, A-Z
	South America
3760	General works
3770	Argentina
3780	Bolivia
3790	Brazil
3800	Chile
3810	Colombia
3820	Ecuador
3831	Guyana
3833	Suriname
3836	French Guiana
3840	Paraguay
3850	Peru

Titles of honor, rank, precedence, etc.
By region or country
South America -- Continued

3860	Uruguay
3870	Venezuela
3880-3889	Europe (Table C20)
3890-3899	Great Britain. England (Table C20)
3900-3909	Scotland (Table C20)
3910-3919	Northern Ireland (Table C20)
3920	Wales
3925-3928	Ireland (Table C21)
3930-3939	Austria (Table C20)
3940-3949	France (Table C20)
3950-3959	Germany (Table C20)
	Including West Germany
3960-3963	East Germany (Table C21)
3966-3969	Greece (Table C21)
3970-3979	Italy (Table C20)
3990-3999	Belgium (Table C20)
4000-4003	Netherlands (Table C21)
4005-4008	Poland (Table C21)
4010-4019	Russia. Former Soviet republics (Table C20)
4020-4023	Czechoslovakia (Table C21)
4025-4028	Hungary (Table C21)
4030-4033	Scandinavia (Table C21)
4035-4038	Denmark (Table C21)
4040-4043	Iceland (Table C21)
4046-4049	Finland (Table C21)
4050-4059	Norway (Table C20)
4060-4069	Sweden (Table C20)
4070-4079	Spain (Table C20)
4080-4089	Portugal (Table C20)
4090-4099	Switzerland (Table C20)
	Balkan States
4100-4103	Albania (Table C21)
4105-4108	Bulgaria (Table C21)
4120-4129	Romania (Table C20)
4130-4133	Yugoslavia (Table C21)
4134-4137	Serbia (Table C21)
	Asia
4150	General works
4153	Turkey
4155	Saudi Arabia
4160-4169	China (Table C20)
4180-4189	India (Table C20)
4190	Sri Lanka
4192	Indonesia

	Titles of honor, rank, precedence, etc.
	By region or country
	Asia -- Continued
4195	Thailand
4200-4209	Japan (Table C20)
4210-4219	Iran (Table C20)
4220	Philippines
4250.A-Z	Other Asian countries, A-Z
4250.I7	Iraq
	Africa
4260	General works
	Egypt
4260.5	Periodicals. Societies. Serials
4261	General works
	History
4262	General works
4263	Early
4264	Medieval
4265	Modern
	Special topics
4266	Usurpation of titles, etc.
4267	Particle of nobility
4268	Order of precedence
4269	Other special (not A-Z)
	Including law of peerage
4280-4283	Ethiopia (Table C21)
4290-4293	Morocco (Table C21)
4300-4303	Nigeria (Table C21)
4310-4313	South Africa (Table C21)
4320.A-Z	Other African countries, A-Z
4330-4339	Australia (Table C20)
4400-4409	New Zealand (Table C20)
4420.A-Z	Pacific islands, A-Z
4420.H3	Hawaiian Islands
	Royalty. Insignia. Regalia, crown and coronets, etc.
	Class here general works only
	For heraldry aspects see CR53
	For royalty of a particular country see CR199+
	Cf. NK7400+ Decorative art
4480	General works
4485.A-Z	Special, A-Z
4485.C7	Crown
4485.O7	Orb
4485.T5	Throne
	Chivalry and knighthood (Orders, decorations, etc.)
4501	Museums. Collections
4505	Dictionaries. Encyclopedias

	Chivalry and knighthood (Orders, decorations, etc.) --
	Continued
	History
4509	General works
	By period
4511	Early
4513	Medieval
4515	Modern
4519	Philosophy. Theory. Relation to other topics
4529.A-Z	By region or country, A-Z
	General works
4531	Through 1800
4533	1801-
4534	General special
4535	Training. Education, etc.
4537	Initiation
4539	Privileges
	Arms and armor (Art) see NK6600+
	Arms and armor (Ethnology) see GN497.5+
	Arms and armor (Military) see U799+
	Ceremonials, pageants, tournaments, etc.
4547	General works
	Celebrations, processions, entertainments
	see classes D, GT
	Coronations, baptisms, marriages, funerals
	see classes D, GT
4553	Tournaments
	Class here general works only
	For works on special tournaments or tournaments of a
	particular region or country, see subclasses D - DU
4565	Wager of battle, trial by ordeal, etc.
	Duels and dueling
4571	Code of honor
	History
4575	General works
4579	General special
4585	Controversial material (Ethics, necessity, results, etc.)
4595.A-Z	By region or country, A-Z

Under each country:

.x	*General works*
.x2A-.x2Z	*Individual cases, A-Z*
	Class here duels having no historic interest
	For duels between public men, see the country and period, e.g.

Orders, etc.

Chivalry and knighthood (Orders, decorations, etc.)
Orders, etc. -- Continued
History and description
General works

4651	Through 1800
4653	1801-
	By period
4657	Early
4659	Medieval
4661	Modern

Rolls of honor. Lists of knights, members of orders, recipients of medals, etc.

4671	General works

By region or country see CR4796.2+
Military-religious orders

4701	General works
4705	General special

International orders

4708	Birgittines. La Sacra milizia del SS. Salvatore o di S. Brigida
4711	Order of Holy Mary, Mother of God
4711.5	Order of Sant'Huberto di Lorena

Orders of St. John of Jerusalem
Including Knights Hospitalers, Knights of Rhodes, and Knights of Malta
Cf. CD5547 Seals (Knights of Malta)
Cf. CJ1693 Numismatics (Knights of Malta)
Cf. CR5563 Papal orders

4715	Sources and documents
4717	Statutes, regulations, etc.
4719	Lists and arms of knights
	History
4723	General works
4725	General special
	Biography
4728	Collective
4729.A-Z	Individual, A-Z
4731.A-Z	By region or country, A-Z

Under each country:

.x	General works
.x2A-.x2Z	Local, A-Z

Order of the Temple (Knights Templars)
Cf. CD5549 Seals
Cf. CJ1695 Numismatics

4735	Sources and documents
4737	Statutes, regulations, etc.
4739	Lists of arms of knights

Chivalry and knighthood (Orders, decorations, etc.)
    Orders, etc.
        Military-religious orders
           International orders
               Order of the Temple (Knights Templars) -- Continued
                History

4743	General works
4749	General special. Suppression of the order
	Biography
4752	Collective
4753.A-Z	Individual, A-Z
4755.A-Z	By region or country, A-Z

                   Under each country (unless otherwise specified):

	.x *General works*
	.x2A-.x2Z *Local, A-Z*

                France

4755.F7	General works
4755.F8A-.F8Z	Local, A-Z
	Great Britain
4755.G7	General works
4755.G8A-.G8Z	Local, A-Z
	Masonic templary see HS741+
	Teutonic Knights
	Cf. CD5551 Seals
	Cf. CJ1697 Numismatics
	Cf. CR4991 Austrian order
4759	Sources and documents
4765	History

                  For the Teutonic Knights in East Prussia see
                      DK4600.P77+
               Teutonic Knights
                Biography

4770	Collective
4771.A-Z	Individual, A-Z
4775.A-Z	By country, German state, etc., A-Z
	e.g.
4775.H4	Hesse
4775.L3	Latvia
	Netherlands
4775.N4	General works
4775.N5A-.N5Z	Local, A-Z
4775.N5U5	Utrecht
4775.W4U5	Westphalia
4785	Ordre sacré impérial angélique de la croix de Constantin-le-Grand
4786	Ordre souverain militaire et dynastique des Chevaliers de la Croix de Constantinople

Chivalry and knighthood (Orders, decorations, etc.)
Orders, etc.
Military-religious orders
International orders -- Continued

4787	Ritter vom Heiligen Grabe
	By region or country
	Europe
	General works see CR4531+
4797	Eastern Europe (General)
	Great Britain
4801	General works
4809	Lists of knights
4815	Knights Bachelor
4819	Order of the Bath
4821	Order of the British Empire
4823	Distinguished Service Order
4827	Order of the Garter
	Royal Hanoverian Guelphic Order see CR5215
4835	Order of St. Michael and St. George
4839	Royal Order of Victoria and Albert
4843	Royal Victorian Order
	Order of British India see CR6050.A2+
4851	Imperial Order of the Crown of India
4855	Order of the Indian Empire
4859	Order of the Star of India
4860	Order of Merit
4869.A-Z	Other orders, A-Z
	Medals and decorations
4871	General works
4875	Albert medal
4880	George Cross
4885	Victoria Cross
4887	George Medal
	Scotland
4901	General works
4905	Knights Bachelor
4909	Order of the Thistle
4917.A-Z	Other orders, A-Z
	Ireland
4925	General works
4929	Knights Bachelor
4933	Order of St. Patrick
4941.A-Z	Other orders, A-Z
	Austria
4951	General works
4955	Lists of knights
4959	Order of Elizabeth Theresa

Chivalry and knighthood (Orders, decorations, etc.)
Orders, etc.
By region or country
Europe
Austria -- Continued

4963	Order of Francis Joseph
4967	Order of the Golden Fleece
4971	Order of the Iron Crown
4975	Order of Leopold
4979	Order of Maria Theresa
4983	Order of St. Stephen
4987	Order of the Starry Cross
4991	Teutonic Knights
5001.A-Z	Other orders, A-Z
5005	Medals and decorations

Czechoslovakia. Czech Republic

5010.A2	General works
5010.A3-Z	Particular orders, A-Z

Slovakia

5011	General works
5012.A-Z	Particular orders, A-Z

Hungary

5015.A2	General works
5015.A3-Z	Particular orders, A-Z

France

5025	General works
5031	List of knights

Royal orders

5035	Order of the Holy Ghost
5037	Order of Our Lady of Mount Carmel and St. Lazarus of Jerusalem
5039	Order of St. Louis
5041	Order of St. Michael
5045.A-Z	Other royal orders, A-Z

Legion of Honor

5055	Constitution and statutes

Lists and biography of members

5059	General works and France
5061.A-Z	Other regions or countries, A-Z
5065	General works
5071	General special
5081.A-Z	Other orders, A-Z
5085	Medals and decorations

Monaco

5095.A2	General works
5095.A3-Z	Particular orders, A-Z

Germany

Chivalry and knighthood (Orders, decorations, etc.)
Orders, etc.
By region or country
Europe
Germany -- Continued

5100	General works
5105	Lists of knights
5109	Medals and decorations
	Anhalt
5115	Order of Albert the Bear
5117.A-Z	Other orders, A-Z
5119	Medals and decorations
	Baden
5125	General works
5129	Order of the Lion of Zähringen
5131	Order of Loyalty, or Fidelity
5133	Order of Military Merit of Charles Frederick
5139.ZA-Z	Other orders, A-Z
	Bavaria
5147	General works
5155	Order of the Bavarian Crown, or of Civil Merit
5157	Order of Elizbeth
5159	Order of Louis
5161	Order of Maximilian
5163	Order of Maximilian Joseph
5165	Order of Military Merit
5167	Order of St. Anne
5169	Order of St. George
5171	Order of St. Hubert
5173	Order of St. Michael
5175	Order of Theresa
5181.A-Z	Other orders, A-Z
5185	Medals and decorations
	Brunswick
5200	Order of Henry the Lion
5205.A-Z	Other orders, A-Z
5206	Medals and decorations
	Hanover
5215	Royal Hanoverian Guelphic Order
5219.A-Z	Other orders, A-Z
	Hesse
5225	General works
5229	Order of the Golden Lion
5231	Order of Louis
5233	Order of Merit of Philip the Magnanimous, or Merit of the House of Philippe-le-Bon
5235	Order of Military Merit

CR

Chivalry and knighthood (Orders, decorations, etc.)
  Orders, etc.
    By region or country
      Europe
        Germany
          Hesse -- Continued

5237	Order of the Military Sanitary Cross
5241.A-Z	Other orders, A-Z
	Lippe. Schaumburg-Lippe
5251	Order of the Cross of Honor
5255.A-Z	Other orders, A-Z
	Mecklenburg-Schwerin. Mecklenburg-Strelitz
5261	Order of the Wendish Crown
5265	Order of the Cross of Military Merit
5267.A-Z	Other orders, A-Z
	Oldenburg
5281	Order of Merit and of the Duke Peter Frederick Louis
5285.A-Z	Other orders, A-Z
	Prussia
5300	General works
5303	Lists of knights
5307	Order of the Black Eagle
5315	Order of the Crown
5319	Order of the House of Hohenzollern
5323	Order of Louisa
	Order "Pour le Mérite"
5327	General works
5329	Arts and sciences
5331	Order of the Red Eagle
5341.A-Z	Other orders, A-Z
	Medals and decorations
5345	General works
5351	Iron Cross
5353	Cross of merit for women and girls
	Reuss
5361	Order of the Cross of Honor
5365.A-Z	Other orders, A-Z
	Saxon duchies
5368	Ernestine Order
	Saxe-Coburg-Gotha
5371	Cross of merit in arts and sciences
5375.A-Z	Other orders, A-Z
	Saxe-Meiningen
5378	Cross of merit in arts and sciences
5379.A-Z	Other orders, A-Z
	Saxe-Weimar-Eisenach

Chivalry and knighthood (Orders, decorations, etc.)
  Orders, etc.
    By region or country
      Europe
        Germany
          Saxe-Weimar-Eisenach -- Continued

5383	Order of the White Falcon
5385.A-Z	Other orders, A-Z
	Saxony
5391	General works
5397	Order of Civil Merit
5400	Order of Merit of Albert the Valorous
5403	Order of the Rue, or Green Crown
5405	Order of St. Henry
5407	Order of Sidonia
5415.A-Z	Other orders, A-Z
5419	Medals and decorations
	Schwarzburg-Rudolstadt. Schwarzburg-Sondershausen
5427	Order of the Cross of Honor
5431.A-Z	Other orders, A-Z
5435	Thuringia
	Waldeck
5441	Order of the Cross of Civil and Military Merit
5445.A-Z	Other orders, A-Z
	Württemberg
5451	General works
5457	Order of the Crown
5459	Order of Frederick
5461	Order of Military Merit
5463	Order of Olga
5471.A-Z	Other orders, A-Z
5475	Medals and decorations
	Greece
5485	General works
5487	Order of the Redeemer (Savior)
5489.A-Z	Other orders, A-Z
	Italy
5500	General works
5507	Order of the Annunciation (Annunziata)
5511	Order of the Crown of Italy, or Iron Crown
5514	Order of Saint Januarius
5515	Order of St. Maurice and St. Lazarus
5519	Order of San Marino
5523	Order of Savoy
5525	Military Order of Savoy
5535.A-Z	Other orders, A-Z

Chivalry and knighthood (Orders, decorations, etc.)
Orders, etc.
By region or country
Europe
Italy -- Continued
5537   Medals and decorations
               Papal orders and decorations
5547   General works
5553   Order of Christ
5555   Order of the Holy Sepulcher
5557   Order of Pius
5559   Order of St. Cecilia
5561   Order of St. Gregory the Great
5563   Order of St. John of Jerusalem
5565   Order of St. Sylvester
5575.A-Z   Other orders, A-Z
5577   Medals and decorations
               Sardinia
5580.A2   General works
5580.A3-Z   Particular orders, A-Z
           Belgium
5590   General works
5595   Order of the Iron Cross, or Order of Civil Merit
5597   Order of Leopold
5605.A-Z   Other orders, A-Z
5607   Medals and decorations
           Netherlands
5617   General works
5625   Order of the Netherlands Lion
5627   Order of Wiliam
5635.A-Z   Other orders, A-Z
5637   Medals and decorations
           Luxembourg
5640   General works
5645   Order of the Golden Lion
5647   Order of the Oak Crown
5649   Medals and decorations
           Russia. Soviet Union. Russia (Federation)
5657   General works
5665   Order of Alexander Nevski
5669   Order of Military Merit
5673   Order of St. Andrew
5677   Order of St. Anne
5681   Order of St. Catherine
5685   Order of St. George
5687   Order of St. Stanislaus
                   Polish before 1831

Chivalry and knighthood (Orders, decorations, etc.)
 Orders, etc.
  By region or country
   Europe
    Russia. Soviet Union. Russia (Federation) --
     Continued

5689	Order of St. Vladimir
5700.A-Z	Other orders, A-Z
5703	Medals and decorations
5707	Geroĭ Sovetskogo Soĭuza. Geroĭ Rossiĭskoĭ Federat͡sii

    Ukraine

5711	General works
5712.A-Z	Individual orders, A-Z

    Poland

5713	General works
5714	Order Budowniczych Polski Ludowej
5716	Order Krżyza Grunwaldu
5719	Order of Military Merit
5721	Order of St. Stanislaus
	Russian since 1831
5723	Order of the White Eagle
	Russian, 1831-1918
5730.A-Z	Other orders, A-Z
5733	Medals and decorations
5737	Virtuti militari

    Livonia

5738	Order of the Brothers of the Sword

    Estonia

5739.A2	General works
5739.A3-Z	Particular orders, A-Z

    Finland

5741.A2	General works
5741.A3-Z	Particular orders, A-Z

    Latvia

5743.A2	General works
5743.A3-Z	Particular orders, A-Z

    Lithuania

5744.A2	General works
5744.A3-Z	Particular orders, A-Z

    Scandinavia

5745	General works

     Denmark

5750	General works
5755	Order of Dannebrog, or Flag of the Danes
5757	Order of the Elephant
5763.A-Z	Other orders, A-Z

Chivalry and knighthood (Orders, decorations, etc.)
  Orders, etc.
    By region or country
      Europe
        Scandinavia
          Denmark -- Continued

5765	Medals and decorations
	Norway
5771	General works
5772	Order of the Norwegian Lion
5775	Order of the St. Olaf
5779.A-Z	Other orders, A-Z
5781	Medals and decorations
	Sweden
5787	General works
5791	Order of Charles XIII
5793	Order of the Pole Star, Polar Star, North Star, or Black Ribbon
5795	Order of the Seraphim, or Blue Ribbon
5797	Order of the Sword, Gauntlet, or Yellow Ribbon
5799	Order of Vasa, or the Green Ribbon
5807.A-Z	Other orders, A-Z
5809	Medals and decorations
5812	Iceland
	Spain
5819	General works
5825	Order of Alcantara
5829	Order of Beneficencia
5833	Order of Calatrava
5837	Order of Charles III, or the Immaculate Conception
5845	Order of Isabella the Catholic
5849	Order of Maria Isabella Louisa
5853	Order of Maria Louisa
5857	Order of Military Merit
5861	Order of Naval Merit
5865	Order of Our Lady of Montesa
5869	Order of St. Ferdinand
5873	Order of St. Hermenegild
5877	Order of St. James of Compostella (Santiago)
5887.A-Z	Other orders, A-Z
5889	Medals and decorations
	Portugal
5900	General works
5907	Order of the Knights of Jesus Christ
5909	Order of Our Lady of the Conception of Villa Vicosa
5911	Order of St. Benedict of Aviz or of Evora
5913	Order of St. Isabella

      Chivalry and knighthood (Orders, decorations, etc.)
       Orders, etc.
        By region or country
         Europe
          Portugal -- Continued

5915	Order of St. James of the Sword
5917	Order of the Tower and the Sword
5923.A-Z	Other orders, A-Z
5925	Medals and decorations
	Switzerland
5935.A2	General works
5935.A3-Z	Particular orders, A-Z
	Balkan States
	Albania
5950.A2	General works
5950.A3-Z	Particular orders, A-Z
	Bulgaria
5955.A2	General works
5955.A3-Z	Particular orders, A-Z
	Croatia
5956.A2	General works
5956.A3-Z	Particular orders, A-Z
	Romania
5975.A2	General works
5975.A3-Z	Particular orders, A-Z
	Yugoslavia
5985.A2	General works
5985.A3-Z	Particular orders, A-Z
	Asia
6000	General works
	Arabia
6010.A2	General works
6010.A3-Z	Particular orders, A-Z
	China
6020.A2	General works
6020.A3-Z	Particular orders, A-Z
	Indonesia
6040.A2	General works
6040.A3-Z	Particular orders, A-Z
	India
6050.A2	General works
6050.A3-Z	Particular orders, A-Z
	Sri Lanka
6060.A2	General works
6060.A3-Z	Particular orders, A-Z
	Thailand
6080.A2	General works

CR

Chivalry and knighthood (Orders, decorations, etc.)
Orders, etc.
By region or country
Asia
Thailand -- Continued
6080.A3-Z   Particular orders, A-Z
Japan
6090.A2   General works
6090.A3-Z   Particular orders, A-Z
Korea
6095.A2   General works
6095.A3-Z   Particular orders, A-Z
Iran
6100.A2   General works
6100.A3-Z   Particular orders, A-Z
Philippines
6120.A2   General works
6120.A3-Z   Particular orders, A-Z
Turkey
6140.A2   General works
6140.A3-Z   Particular orders, A-Z
6150.A-Z   Other divisions of Asia, A-Z
     e.g.
6150.S5   Singapore
Africa
6160   General works
Egypt
6170.A2   General works
6170.A3-Z   Particular orders, A-Z
South Africa
6180.A2   General works
6180.A3-Z   Particular orders, A-Z
6190.A-Z   Other African divisions, A-Z
     e.g.
6190.M3   Madagascar
Australia
6220.A2A-.A2Z   General works
6220.A3-Z   Particular orders, A-Z
New Zealand
6230.A2   General works
6230.A3-Z   Particular orders, A-Z
6240.A-Z   Pacific islands, A-Z
6240.H3   Hawaiian Islands
North America
6250   General works
6253   United States
6257   Canada

Chivalry and knighthood (Orders, decorations, etc.)
Orders, etc.
By region or country
North America -- Continued

6261	Mexico
6265	Central America
6267	West Indies
	South America
6270	General works
6273	Argentina
6275	Bolivia
6277	Brazil
6287	Chile
6289	Colombia
6291	Ecuador
6293	French Guiana
6295	Guyana
6297	Paraguay
6299	Peru
6301	Suriname
6303	Uruguay
6305	Venezuela

	Genealogy
	For family archives see CD1+
1	Periodicals. Societies. Serials
2	Congresses
	Collected works (nonserial)
3	Several authors
4	Individual authors
5	Directories
6	Dictionaries. Encyclopedias
7	History
	Biography of genealogists
8.A1	Collective
8.A2-Z	Individual, A-Z
	e.g.
8.D3	Deane, W. R.
8.W5	Whitmore, W. H.
8.5	Certification of genealogists
	General works
9	American and English
10	French
11	German
12	Other languages (not A-Z)
14	General special
15.5	Juvenile works
	Popular works
	Including pedigree tracing, writing a family history, etc.
16	American and English
17	French
18	German
19	Other languages (not A-Z)
21	General special
21.5	Computer network resources
	Including Internet resources
22	Cemetery records
	For specific countries see CS42+
23	Lists and manuals of unclaimed estates
24	Charts, forms, diagrams, etc.
	Genealogical lists, etc., covering more than one country or continent
25	General works
	By class
27	Royalty, ruling families, chief magistrates, etc.
	e.g. Almanach de Gotha
28	Nobility
29	Gentry
30	Commoners
31	Other classes (not A-Z)

	Genealogical lists, etc., covering more than one country or
	continent -- Continued
	By period
33	Early
34	Medieval
35	Modern
36.A-Z	Special topics, A-Z
	For list of Cutter numbers for special topics, see Table C22 16
	Family history covering more than one country
	For works that include the United States see CS69+
38	Collective
39.A-Z	Individual, A-Z
	Under each:
	.x *Periodicals. Serials*
	.x2 *General works. By date*
	By region or country
	United States
	For local genealogy of the United States, see the place in class
	F, e.g. F180 Maryland; F189.B1 Baltimore
	For genealogy of particular ethnic groups, see the group in
	classes E-F, e.g. E184.G3, German Americans
42	Periodicals. Societies. Serials
42.7	Sources and documents
	Collected works (nonserial)
43	Several authors
43.5	Individual authors
44	Directories
45	Dictionaries. Encyclopedias
47	General works
49	General special
	By class
	Royalty and nobility
55	By descent
57	By marriage. Titled Americans
59	Other (not A-Z)
	By period
61	Colonial
63	Revolutionary
65	Later
66.A-Z	Special topics, A-Z
	For list of Cutter numbers for special topics, see Table C22
	16
	Records
	Including wills, sepulchral records, registers of marriages,
	births, deaths, etc.
	For contested will cases, see class K
68	General collections

CS

	By region or country	
	United States	
	Records -- Continued	
	Local	
	see class F	
	Family history	
69	Collective	
71.A-Z	Individual, A-Z	
	Under each:	
	.x	*Periodicals. Serials*
	.x2	*General works. By date*
	Cf. CT274.A+ Biography	
	Canada	
80	Periodicals. Societies. Serials	
81	Directories	
82	General works	
83	General special	
	By class	
84	Royalty and nobility in general	
85	Commoners	
	By period	
86	Early	
87	Modern	
	Special topics see CS83	
	Local (Not elsewhere provided for)	
	Including wills, sepulchral records, registers of marriages, births, deaths, etc.	
	For contested will cases, see class K	
88.A1	Collective	
88.A3-Z	By province (or other subdivision), A-Z	
	Family history	
89	Collective	
90.A-Z	Individual, A-Z	
	Under each:	
	.x	*Periodicals. Serials*
	.x2	*General works. By date*
93	Greenland	
	Latin America	
95	General works	
	Mexico	
100	Periodicals. Societies. Serials	
101	Directories	
102	General works	
103	General special	
	By class	
104	Royalty and nobility in general	
105	Commoners	

By region or country
Latin America
Mexico -- Continued
By period
106   Early
107   Modern
Special topics see CS103
Local (Not elsewhere provided for)
Including wills, sepulchral records, registers of marriages, births, deaths, etc.
For contested will cases, see class K
108.A1   Collective
108.A3-Z   By province (or other subdivision), A-Z
Family history
109   Collective
110.A-Z   Individual, A-Z

Under each:

.x	*Periodicals. Serials*
.x2	*General works. By date*

Central America
120-129   General (Table C23)
130-139   Belize (Table C23)
140-149   Costa Rica (Table C23)
150-159   Guatemala (Table C23)
160-169   Honduras (Table C23)
170-179   Nicaragua (Table C23)
180-189   Panama (Table C23)
190-199   El Salvador (Table C23)
West Indies
200-209   General (Table C23)
210-219   Bahamas (Table C23)
220-229   Cuba (Table C23)
230-239   Haiti (Table C23)
240-249   Jamaica (Table C23)
250-259   Puerto Rico (Table C23)
261.A-Z   Other. By island or group of islands, A-Z

Under each:

.x	*Collective. By author, A-Z*
.x2	*Individual. By family and date*

South America
270-279   General (Table C23)
280-289   Argentina (Table C23)
290-299   Bolivia (Table C23)
300-309   Brazil (Table C23)
310-319   Chile (Table C23)
320-329   Colombia (Table C23)
330-339   Ecuador (Table C23)

	By region or country
	Latin America
	South America -- Continued
339.5	French Guiana
340-349	Suriname (Table C23)
350-359	Guyana (Table C23)
360-369	Paraguay (Table C23)
370-379	Peru (Table C23)
380-389	Uruguay (Table C23)
390-399	Venezuela (Table C23)
	Europe
400-409	General (Table C23)
409.5	Eastern Europe (General)
	Great Britain. England
410	Periodicals. Societies. Serials
410.7	Sources and documents
	Collective works (nonserial)
411	Several authors
411.5	Individual authors
412	Directories
413	Dictionaries. Encyclopedias
414	General works
415	General special
	By class
418	Royalty. Royal descent
419	Nobility in general. Armorial families
	Class here general visitations; for special visitations, see CS437
	Titled nobility
420	General works
	Peerage (Baronage)
421	General works
422	Extinct and dormant
	Claims
423.A2	Collections
423.A3-Z	Individual, A-Z
424	Baronetage
	Untitled nobility. Gentry
425	General works
426	Commoners
	By period
428	Early
429	Medieval
430	Modern
432.A-Z	Special groups. By occupation, religion, origin, etc., A-Z
432.A57	Airmen
432.B34	Baptists

By region or country
　　Europe
　　　Great Britain. England
　　　　Special groups. By occupation, religion, origin, etc., A-Z -
　　　　　　- Continued

432.B73	Brewers
432.C36	Catholics
432.C62	Coal miners
432.D56	Dissenters
432.F74	French
432.H8	Huguenot families
432.J4	Jews
432.M3	Marshalls
432.M46	Merchant mariners
432.M48	Methodists
432.N7	Norman families
432.P3	Palatines
432.P6	Police
432.P67	Poor
432.P7	Priests
432.R34	Railroad employees
432.R64	Romanies
432.S25	Sailors
432.S3	Scots
432.S5	Sheriffs
432.S64	Soldiers

　　　　Records
　　　　　Including wills, sepulchral records, registers of marriages,
　　　　　　births, deaths, etc.
　　　　　For contested will cases, see class K
　　　　　For history and description of parish registers see
　　　　　　CD1068.A2+

434	General collections
	Local
435.A-Z	Counties, regions, etc., A-Z
435.A9	Avon
435.B3	Bedfordshire
435.B5	Berkshire
435.B8	Buckinghamshire
435.C2	Cambridgeshire (Pre-1965; Post-1974)
435.C3	Cambridgeshire and Isle of Ely (1965-1974)
435.C5	Cheshire
435.C55	Cleveland
435.C6	Cornwall
435.C8	Cumberland
435.C9	Cumbria
435.D2	Derbyshire

CS

By region or country
Europe
Great Britain. England
Records
Local
Counties, regions, etc., A-Z -- Continued

435.D35	Devonshire
435.D6	Dorsetshire
435.D8	Durham
435.E3	East Sussex
435.E7	Essex
435.G5	Gloucestershire
435.H2	Hampshire
435.H3	Hereford and Worcester
435.H4	Herefordshire
435.H6	Hertfordshire
435.H7	Humberside
435.H8	Huntingdonshire
435.K5	Kent
435.L3	Lancashire
435.L5	Leicestershire
435.L7	Lincolnshire
	London see CS436.L7A1+
435.M3	Merseyside
435.M4	Middlesex
435.M53	Midlands
435.N2	Norfolk
435.N25	North Yorkshire
435.N4	Northamptonshire
435.N6	Northumberland
435.N8	Nottinghamshire
435.O9	Oxfordshire
435.R8	Rutlandshire
435.S2	Salop. Shropshire
	Shropshire see CS435.S2
435.S3	Somersetshire
435.S35	South East
435.S4	South Yorkshire
	Southhamption (County) see CS435.H2
435.S5	Staffordshire
435.S7	Suffolk
435.S8	Surrey
435.S9	Sussex
435.T9	Tyne and Wear
435.W2	Warwickshire
	Wear see CS435.T9
435.W37	West Country

	By region or country
	Europe
	Great Britain. England
	Records
	Local
	Counties, regions, etc., A-Z -- Continued
435.W4	West Midlands
435.W43	West Sussex
435.W45	West Yorkshire
435.W5	Westmorland
435.W6	Wiltshire
	Worcester see CS435.H3
435.W8	Worcestershire
435.Y4	Yorkshire
436.A-Z	Parishes, cities, etc., A-Z
	e.g.
436.B58	Birmingham
436.C4	Canterbury
436.I6	Ipswich
436.L5	Lincoln
	London
436.L7A1-.A23	Documents
436.L7A25-.A55	General works. By author or editor (alphabetically)
436.L7A65-Z	Special parishes, institutions, etc., A-Z
436.L7A7	All Hallows
436.L7A8	St. Anne's
436.L7B6	St. Botolph
436.L7B85	Bunhill Fields
436.L7D65	Draper's Co.
436.L7G5	Gray's Inn
436.L7W67	Worshipful Company of Parish Clerks
436.M24	Manchester
436.O4	Oldham
436.R6	Rochdale
436.S68	St. Michael's on Wyre
436.S87	Suffolk
437.A-Z	County visitations. By county, A-Z
	Family history
438	Collective
439.A-Z	Individual, A-Z
	Under each:
	.x · *Periodicals. Serials*
	.x2 · *General works. By date*
440-449	Northern Ireland (Table C23)
450-459	Wales (Table C23)
460-479	Scotland (Table C22)

By region or country
　Europe
　　Great Britain. England -- Continued
479.5　　　　　　　　Isle of Man
479.7　　　　　　　　Channel Islands
480-499　　　　　　Ireland (Table C22)
500-519　　　　　　Austria (Table C22)
520-539　　　　　　Czechoslovakia. Czech Republic (Table C22)
540-549　　　　　　Slovakia (Table C23)
560-569　　　　　　Hungary (Table C23)
580-599　　　　　　France (Table C22)
610-629　　　　　　Germany (Table C22 modified)
　　　　　　　　　　　Including West Germany
　　　　　　　　　By class
616　　　　　　　　　Royalty and court
　　　　　　　　　　Nobility
617　　　　　　　　　　General works
618　　　　　　　　　　Counts (Gräfliche familien)
619　　　　　　　　　　Barons (Freiherrliche familien)
620　　　　　　　　　　Lesser nobility (Adelige familien)
621　　　　　　　　　　Commoners (Bürgerliche familien)
680-699　　　　　　East Germany (Table C22)
730-739　　　　　　Greece (Table C23)
750-769　　　　　　Italy (Table C22)
(762)　　　　　　　　Roman noble families
　　　　　　　　　　　　see DG204
772　　　　　　　　Malta
775　　　　　　　　San Marino (Republic)
778　　　　　　　　Liechtenstein
780-789　　　　　　Low countries (Table C23)
790-809　　　　　　Belgium (Table C22)
810-829　　　　　　Netherlands (Table C22)
830-839　　　　　　Luxembourg (Table C23)
840-859　　　　　　Russia. Former Soviet republics (Table C22)
　　　　　　　　Belarus
859.2　　　　　　　General works
　　　　　　　　　Local
859.23　　　　　　　Collective
859.24.A-Z　　　　　By province (or other subdivision), A-Z
　　　　　　　　　Family history
859.25　　　　　　　Collective
859.3.A-Z　　　　　　Individual, A-Z
　　　　　　　　Moldova
859.6　　　　　　　General works
　　　　　　　　　Local
859.63　　　　　　　Collective
859.64.A-Z　　　　　By province (or other subdivision), A-Z

	By region or country
	Europe
	Moldova -- Continued
	Family history
859.65	Collective
859.7.A-Z	Individual, A-Z
860-869	Ukraine (Table C23)
870-879	Poland (Table C23)
	Baltic States
	Estonia
879.2	General works
	Family history
879.25	Collective
879.3.A-Z	Individual, A-Z
	Latvia
879.4	General works
	Family history
879.45	Collective
879.5.A-Z	Individual, A-Z
	Lithuania
879.6	General works
	Family history
879.65	Collective
879.7.A-Z	Individual, A-Z
880-889	Finland (Table C23)
890-899	Scandinavia (Table C23)
900-909	Denmark (Table C23)
910-919	Norway (Table C23)
920-929	Sweden (Table C23)
930-939	Iceland (Table C23)
940-959	Spain (Table C22)
960-969	Portugal (Table C23)
980-999	Switzerland (Table C22)
1000-1009	Balkan States (Table C23)
1010-1019	Albania (Table C23)
	Bosnia and Hercegovina
1019.5	General works
	Family history
1019.55	Collective
1019.6.A-Z	Individual, A-Z
1020-1029	Bulgaria (Table C23)
1030-1039	Croatia (Table C23)
1039.5	Macedonia (Republic)
	Montenegro
1039.7	General works
	Family history
1039.75	Collective

By region or country
Europe
Balkan States
Montenegro
Family history -- Continued

1039.8.A-Z	Individual, A-Z
1040-1049	Romania (Table C23)
1049.5	Slovenia
1050-1059	Yugoslavia. Serbia (Table C23)
	Asia
1080-1089	General (Table C23)
1095	Near East
1096	Armenia (Republic)
1097	Azerbaijan
1098	Georgia (Republic)
1100-1109	Afghanistan (Table C23)
1120-1129	Saudi Arabia (Table C23)
1131	Kuwait
1133	Bahrain
1134	Qatar
1135	United Arab Emirates. Trucial states
1136	Oman
1137	Yemen (People's Democratic Republic)
1138	Yemen
	Central Asia
1139	General works
1139.3	Kazakstan
1139.4	Kyrgyzstan
1139.5	Tajikistan
1139.6	Turkmenistan
1139.7	Uzbekistan
1140-1149	Pakistan (Table C23)
1160-1169	China (Table C23 modified)
	Local
1168.A1	Collective
1168.A3-Z	By province (or other subdivision), A-Z
	e. g.
1168.H85	Hong Kong
1168.M33	Macau
(1169.3)	Macau
	see CS1168.M33
1169.5	Taiwan
(1169.55)	Hong Kong
	see CS1168.H85
1170-1179	Indonesia (Table C23)
1200-1209	India (Table C23)
1210-1219	Sri Lanka (Table C23)

By region or country
   Asia -- Continued

1220-1229	Nepal (Table C23)
1230-1239	Vietnam (Table C23)
1240-1249	Burma (Table C23)
1250-1259	Thailand (Table C23)
1270-1279	Malaysia (Table C23)
1281	Singapore
1300-1309	Japan (Table C23)
1330-1339	Korea (Table C23)
1360-1369	Mongolia (Table C23)
1390-1399	Philippines (Table C23)
1410-1419	Iran (Table C23)
1420-1429	Cyprus (Table C23)
1470-1479	Turkey (Table C23)
1500-1509	Israel (Table C23)
1510-1519	Syria (Table C23)
1520-1529	Iraq (Table C23)
1530-1539	Jordan (Table C23)
1540-1549	Lebanon (Table C23)
1549.5	Arab countries
	Africa
1550-1559	General (Table C23)
1570-1579	Ethiopia (Table C23)
1590-1599	South Africa (Table C23)
1620-1629	Zimbabwe (Table C23)
1647	Zaire
1650-1659	Egypt (Table C23)
1670-1679	Algeria (Table C23)
1680-1689	Tunisia (Table C23)
1690	Benin
1691	Congo
1693	Madagascar
	Mauritius see CS1991.M38
1695	Senegal
1695.5	Mali
1697	Sudan
1699	Nigeria
1710	Cameroon
1711	Tanzania
1718	Somalia
1720-1729	Liberia (Table C23)
1740-1749	Morocco (Table C23)
1770-1779	Libya (Table C23)
	Indian Ocean islands
1990	General
1991.A-Z	Individual islands or groups of islands, A-Z

	By region or country
	Indian Ocean islands
	Individual islands or groups of islands, A-Z -- Continued
1991.M38	Mauritius
1991.R48	Réunion
2000-2009	Australia (Table C23)
2170-2179	New Zealand (Table C23)
	Pacific islands
2191	General
2195.A-Z	Individual islands or groups of islands, A-Z
2200-2209	Hawaiian Islands (Table C23)
	Personal and family names
	For works dealing collectively with personal, geographic, and
	other names, see subclasses P - PM
	For place names and names in individual preliterate societies,
	see classes D - F
	Cf. BF1891.N3 Fortune-telling by names
	Cf. GN468.45 Names and naming systems of preliterate
	and folk societies (General)
	Cf. GT471 House names
2300	Periodicals. Societies. Serials
	Collected works (nonserial)
2301	Several authors
2302	Individual authors
2303	Philological treatises
2305	General works
	Including origin, history, description, etc.
2309	General special
	Legal changes of names. Lists, etc.
	Cf. CR3499+ Titles of honor, rank, precedence, etc.
2325	General works
2327.A-Z	By region or country, A-Z
	By period
	Ancient
	For Asian see CS2950+
	For Egyptian see CS3070
2347	General works
2349	Greek
2351	Roman
2353	Other (not A-Z)
2355	Medieval
2357	Modern
	Forenames Christian names)
	Including masculine names
2367	General works
	Feminine names
2369	General works

Personal and family names
    Forenames
        Feminine names -- Continued

2371.A-Z	By region or country, A-Z
2375.A-Z	By region or country, A-Z
2377	General special
	Including lists of children's names

    Surnames
      Including family names

2385	General works
2389	General special
2391.A-Z	Particular names, A-Z
	e.g.
2391.B4	Benedictus

    By country, nationality, etc.
      Celtic

2395	General works
2398	Breton (Table C24)
2400-2409	Cornish (Table C25)
2410-2419	Irish (Table C25)
2420-2429	Manx (Table C25)
2430-2439	Scotch (Table C25)
2440-2449	Welsh (Table C25)

      Teutonic

2465	General works
2468	Gothic (Table C24)
2470	Anglo-Saxon (Table C24)
2480-2489	American (Table C25)
	For Indian names, see E98.N2; F1219.3.N2; etc.
2500-2509	English (Table C25)
2520-2529	Dutch. Flemish (Table C25)
2529	Local, A-Z
2529.N5	New Netherlands (New York)
2540-2549	German (Table C25)
2560-2569	Scandinavian (Table C25)
2570-2579	Danish (Table C25)
2580	Icelandic (Table C24)
2590-2599	Norwegian (Table C25)
2600-2609	Swedish (Table C25)
2620-2629	Swiss (Table C25)
2640.A-Z	Other, A-Z

      Romance

2685	General works
2690-2699	French (Table C25)
2700	French-Canadian (Table C24)
2710-2719	Italian (Table C25)
2730-2739	Romanian (Table C25)

	Personal and family names
	By country, nationality, etc.
	Romance -- Continued
2740-2749	Spanish (Table C25)
2760-2769	Portuguese (Table C25)
2770.A-Z	Other, A-Z
2770.C3	Catalan
2770.L33	Ladin
	Slavic
2805	General works
2808	Old Slavonic (Table C24)
2810-2819	Russian (Table C25)
	Including non-Russian names of Russia or the Soviet Union
2830	Czech (Table C24)
2840	Polish (Table C24)
2850	Serbo-Croatian (Table C24)
2860.A-Z	Other, A-Z
2860.B44	Belarusian
2860.B8	Bulgarian
2860.M33	Macedonian
2860.U4	Ukrainian
2880	Lithuanian (Table C24)
2900	Finnish (Table C24)
2910	Hungarian (Table C24)
2920	Greek (Modern) (Table C24)
2930	Albanian (Table C24)
2940.A-Z	Other European, A-Z
2940.B37	Basque
	Asian
2950	General works
2955	Semitic (Table C24)
2970	Arabic. Islamic (Table C24)
2980	Armenian (Table C24)
2983	Caucasian (Table C24)
	Including individual Caucasian languages
2990	Chinese (Table C24)
3000	Japanese (Table C24)
3010	Jewish (Table C24)
	Cf. BM729.N3 The name "Jew," "Israel," etc.
3012	Korean (Table C24)
3020	Persian (Table C24)
3030	Sanskrit and other Indic (Table C24)
3040	Turkish (Table C24)
3050.A-Z	Other, A-Z
3050.B37	Bashkir
3050.B8	Burmese
3050.C34	Cambodian

	Personal and family names
	By country, nationality, etc.
	Asian
	Other, A-Z -- Continued
3050.K39	Kazakh
3050.K87	Kurdish
3050.T35	Tatar
3050.T45	Thai
3050.U93	Uzbek
3050.V5	Vietnamese
3070	Egyptian (Table C24)
3080.A-Z	Other African, A-Z
	For works on traditional names of particular African preliterate peoples, see the people in class DT
3080.A4	Amharic
3080.H3	Hausa
3080.K33	Kabyle
3080.M66	Mooré
3080.N5	Nigerian
3080.S9	Swahili
3090.A-Z	Malayo-Polynesian, A-Z
3090.I5	Indonesian

Biography
> Class here general collective or individual biography only. For collective or individual biography representative of special classes or subjects of the classification system, see the class or subject, including H57+ Social scientists; TA139+ Engineers
>
> Cf. Z1010 Bio-bibliography

Biography as an art or literary form

21	General works
22	Technique

> Cf. D16.16 Psychohistory

25	Autobiography

> Cf. PN4390 Diaries (Literary history)

History of biographical literature. Lives of biographers
> For works about biographical literature applicable to special fields, or biographies of biographers concentrating in special fields, see the field, including D13+ Historiography (General history)

31	General works
34.A-Z	By region or country, A-Z
	Ancient
35	General works
37	Oriental
	Classical
	see subclass PA
61	Medieval
	Modern
71	General works
73	15th century
75	16th century
77	17th century
79	18th century
81	19th century
83	20th century
	Study and teaching. Research
85	General works
86	Audiovisual aids
86.Z9	Catalogs
	General collective biography
	Universal in scope. By language
88	Polyglot
93	Latin
	Including Giovio
95	Other early works
	Including Bayle
	American and English
100	Periodicals. Societies. Serials
101	Collected works (nonserial)
	Including "Little journeys," "Famous autobiographies"

CT

General collective biography
  Universal in scope. By language
    American and English -- Continued

102	Early works through 1800
103	Dictionaries. Encyclopedias
104	General works, 1801-
105	General special

       Including men and women who have failed; deaths of
         celebrated men and women

107	Juvenile works
108	Sobriquets and nicknames
109	Humor, satire, etc.

    By period
     Ancient

113	General works

      Classical see DE7
       Plutarch's lives (English translation) see DE7.P5
       Plutarch's lives see PA4369.A2+

114	Medieval

     Modern
      For Yearbooks see CT100

115	15th century
116	16th century
117	17th century
118	18th century
119	19th century
120	20th century

    Individual families, A-Z
  Dutch

130	Periodicals. Societies. Serials
131	Collected works (nonserial)
132	Early works through 1800
133	Dictionaries. Encyclopedias
134	General works, 1801-
135	Juvenile works

    By period

136	Through 1600 (modern works only)

      For ancient and medieval periods see D106+

137	17th-18th centuries
138	19th-20th centuries
139	20th century

  French

140	Periodicals. Societies. Serials
141	Collected works (nonserial)
142	Early works through 1800

     For Bayle see CT95

143	Dictionaries. Encyclopedias

CT

General collective biography
Universal in scope. By language
French -- Continued
144   General works, 1801-
145   Juvenile works
145.3   Sobriquets and nicknames
             By period
146   Through 1600 (modern works only)
                     For ancient and medieval periods see D106+
147   17th and 18th centuries
148   19th and 20th centuries
149   20th century
German
150   Periodicals. Societies. Serials
151   Collected works (nonserial)
152   Early works through 1800
153   Dictionaries. Encyclopedias
154   General works, 1801-
155   Juvenile works
             By period
156   Through 1600 (modern works only)
                     For ancient and medieval periods see D106+
157   17th and 18th centuries
158   19th and 20th centuries
159   20th century
Italian
160   Periodicals. Societies. Serials
161   Collected works (nonserial)
162   Early works through 1800
163   Dictionaries. Encyclopedias
164   General works, 1801-
165   Juvenile works
             By period
166   Through 1600 (modern works only)
                     For ancient and medieval periods see D106+
167   17th and 18th centuries
168   19th and 20th centuries
169   20th century
Scandinavian
170   Periodicals. Societies. Serials
171   Collected works (nonserial)
172   Early works through 1800
173   Dictionaries. Encyclopedias
174   General works, 1801-
175   Juvenile works
             By period

	General collective biography
	Universal in scope. By language
	Scandinavian
	By period -- Continued
176	Through 1600 (modern works only)
	For ancient and medieval periods see D106+
177	17th and 18th centuries
178	19th and 20th centuries
179	20th century
	Spanish and Portuguese
180	Periodicals. Societies. Serials
181	Collected works (nonserial)
182	Early works through 1800
183	Dictionaries. Encyclopedias
184	General works, 1801-
185	Juvenile works
	By period
186	Through 1600 (modern works only)
	For ancient and medieval periods see D106+
187	17th and 18th centuries
188	19th and 20th centuries
189	20th century
	Slavic
190	Periodicals. Societies. Serials
191	Collected works (nonserial)
192	Early works through 1800
193	Dictionaries. Encyclopedias
194	General works, 1801-
195	Juvenile works
	By period
196	Through 1600 (modern works only)
	For ancient and medieval periods see D106+
197	17th and 18th centuries
198	19th and 20th centuries
199	20th century
203.A-Z	Other languages, A-Z
205	General special
	Including collective biography of miscellaneous groups not provided for under CT9960+
	Autographs see Z41.A2+
206	Portraits
	Cf. N7575+ Fine arts
	National biography
	For biographies of persons in public life, see classes D - F
	For literary biography, see class P
	By region or country
	America

CT

	National biography
	By region or country
	America -- Continued
208	General works
	North America
	United States
210	Periodicals. Societies. Serials
211	Collected works (nonserial)
213	Dictionaries. Encyclopedias
214	General works
215	General special
216	Addresses, essays, lectures
217	Juvenile works
217.5	Portraits
	Class here works emphasizing biographical aspects
	For works emphasing the artistic aspects or the artist, see class N
	By period
218	Through 1800
219	19th century
220	20th century
	By region or state
	Class here collective biographies of persons associated with particular states or with particular regions or divisions of a state (except cities)
221	Alabama
222	Alaska
223	Arizona
224	Arkansas
225	California
226	Colorado
226.5	Connecticut
227	Delaware
	District of Columbia see F193
229	Florida
230	Georgia
230.5	Hawaii
231	Idaho
232	Illinois
233	Indiana
234	Iowa
235	Kansas
236	Kentucky
237	Louisiana
238	Maine
239	Maryland
240	Massachusetts

CT

	National biography
	By region or country
	America
	North America
	United States -- Continued
	African American biography (General) see E185.96+
	African American biography (Slavery) see E444
	African American biography (Abolition) see E449+
	Canada
280	Periodicals. Societies. Serials
281	Collected works (nonserial)
283	Dictionaries. Encyclopedias
284	General works
285	Addresses, essays, lectures
285.7	Portraits
	By period
286	Through 1800
287	19th century
288	20th century
	By province
289	Newfoundland
290	Nova Scotia
291	New Brunswick
292	Prince Edward Island
293	Quebec
294	Ontario
295	Manitoba
296	British Columbia
297	Saskatchewan
299	Alberta
	Northwest Territories
301	General works
302	Franklin
303	Keewatin
304	Mackenzie
308	Yukon
	By city
	see class F
309.A-Z	Individual families, A-Z
310.A-Z	Individual persons, A-Z
	Subarrange each by Table C30
	For individual biographies of persons associated with particular cities, see class F
	Mexico see CT550+
	Caribbean
329	General works
330-338	Bermuda (Table C27)

National biography
By region or country
America
Caribbean -- Continued
West Indies

339	General works
339.5	Antigua
340-348	Bahamas (Table C27)
350-350.8	Barbardos (Table C28)
350.9	Cayman Islands
	Cuba see CT510+
351-351.8	Dominica (Table C28)
	Dominican Republic see CT540+
352	Grenada
354	Guadeloupe
	Haiti see CT530+
360-368	Jamaica (Table C27)
372	Martinique
374	Montserrat
	Puerto Rico see CT520+
379	Saint Lucia
379.2	Saint Martin
379.5	Saint Vincent
380-388	Trinidad and Tobago (Table C27)
390-398	Virgin Islands (British) (Table C27)
400-408	Virgin Islands (U.S.) (Table C27)
430-438	Bonaire (Table C27)
440-448	Curaçao (Table C27)
500-506	Latin America (Table C27a)
510-518	Cuba (Table C27)
520-528	Puerto Rico (Table C27)
530-538	Haiti (Table C27)
540-548	Dominican Republic (Table C27)
550-558	Mexico (Table C27)
	Central America
570	General works
580-588	Costa Rica (Table C27)
590-598	Guatemala (Table C27)
600-608	Honduras (Table C27)
609	Belize
610-618	Nicaragua (Table C27)
620-628	Panama (Table C27)
630-638	El Salvador (Table C27)
	South America
640	General works
650-658	Argentina (Table C27)
670-678	Bolivia (Table C27)

CT

	National biography
	By region or country
	America
	Latin America
	South America -- Continued
680-688	Brazil (Table C27)
690-698	Chile (Table C27)
700-708	Colombia (Table C27)
710-718	Ecuador (Table C27)
719	French Guiana
	Guyana
719.5	Collective
719.6.A-Z	Individual, A-Z
	Subarrange each by Table C30
720-728	Paraguay (Table C27)
730-738	Peru (Table C27)
739	Suriname
740-748	Uruguay (Table C27)
750-758	Venezuela (Table C27)
	Europe
759	General works
765	Eastern Europe (General)
769	Commonwealth of Nations
770-788	Great Britain. England (Table C26)
790-808	Northern Ireland (Table C26)
810-828	Scotland (Table C26)
830-848	Wales (Table C26)
850-858	Gibraltar (Table C27)
860-868	Ireland (Table C27)
870-878	Malta (Table C27)
900-918	Austria (Table C26)
930-948	Czechoslovakia. Czech Republic (Table C26)
	Slovakia
949	Collective
949.5.A-Z	Individual, A-Z
	Subarrange each by Table C30
950-968	Hungary (Table C26)
970-978	Liechtenstein (Table C27)
1000-1018	France (Table C26)
1018.A-Z	Individual persons, A-Z
	For individual biographies of political or historical persons, or of persons associated with particular cities, see classes D-F
1018.S45-Z	Schweitzer, Albert

	National biography
	By region or country
	Europe
	France
	Individual, A-Z
	Cf. B2430.S37+ Schweitzer as philosopher
	Cf. BX4827.S35 Schweitzer as theologian
	Cf. ML416.S33 Schweitzer as musician
	Cf. R722.32.S35 Schweitzer as missionary
1020-1028	Andorra (Table C27)
1030-1038	Monaco (Table C27)
	Germany
	Including West Germany
1050	Periodicals. Societies. Serials
1051	Collected works (nonserial)
1052	Early works through 1800
1053	Dictionaries. Encyclopedias
1054	General works, 1801-
1055	General special
1057	Juvenile works
1057.5	Portraits
	By period
	Ancient
	see class D
	Medieval
	see class D
	Modern
1060	15th-16th centuries
1061	17th-18th centuries
1062	19th-20th centuries
1063	20th century
1064	Colonies
	see CT280+
1067	Anhalt
1068	Baden-Württemberg
1069	Bavaria
1070	Bremen
1072	Hamburg
1074	Hesse
1075	Lower Saxony
1079	North Rhine-Westphalia
1080	Prussia
1082	Rhineland-Palatinate
1084	Saarland
1088	Schleswig-Holstein
1093.A-Z	Other states (extinct, mediatized, etc.) and regions, A-Z
	Rulers see DD1+

CT

	National biography
	By region or country
	Europe
	Germany -- Continued
1097.A-Z	Individual families, A-Z
1098.A-Z	Individual persons, A-Z
1099-1099.8	East Germany (Table C28)
1100-1118	Greece (Table C26)
1120-1138	Italy (Table C26)
1139	Low Countries
1140-1158	Netherlands (Table C26)
1160-1178	Belgium (Table C26)
	Luxembourg
1180	Collective
1182.A-Z	Individual, A-Z
	Subarrange each by Table C30
(1195)	Eastern Europe
	see CT765
1200-1218	Russia (Table C26)
	Cf. CT1770+ Soviet Union in Asia
	Finland
1220	Collective
1222.A-Z	Individual, A-Z
	Subarrange each by Table C30
	Belarus
1223	Collective
1223.5.A-Z	Individual, A-Z
	Subarrange each by Table C30
	Moldova
1224	Collective
1224.5.A-Z	Individual, A-Z
	Subarrange each by Table C30
	Ukraine
1225	Collective
1225.5.A-Z	Individual, A-Z
	Subarrange each by Table C30
	Poland
1230	General works
1231.A-Z	Local divisions, A-Z
	For political or historical persons see DK4600+
1231.5.A-Z	Individual families, A-Z
1232.A-Z	Individual persons, A-Z
	Subarrange each by Table C30
	Baltic States
1232.5	General works
	Estonia
1233	Collective

National biography
By region or country
Europe
Baltic States
Estonia -- Continued
1233.5.A-Z   Individual, A-Z
Subarrange each by Table C30
Latvia
1234   Collective
1234.5.A-Z   Individual, A-Z
Subarrange each by Table C30
Lithuania
1235   Collective
1235.5.A-Z   Individual, A-Z
Subarrange each by Table C30
1240-1258   Scandinavia (Table C26)
1260-1278   Denmark (Table C26)
Iceland
1280   Collective
1282.A-Z   Individual, A-Z
Subarrange each by Table C30
1290-1308   Norway (Table C26)
1310-1328   Sweden (Table C26)
1340-1358   Spain (Table C26)
1360-1378   Portugal (Table C26)
1380-1398   Switzerland (Table C26)
Balkan States
Albania
1399   Collective
1399.2.A-Z   Individual, A-Z
Subarrange each by Table C30
Bosnia and Hercegovina
1399.5   Collective
1399.52.A-Z   Individual, A-Z
Subarrange each by Table C30
1400-1408   Bulgaria (Table C27)
1410-1418   Croatia (Table C27)
1420-1428   Macedonia (Republic) (Table C27)
1430-1438   Romania (Table C27)
1440-1448   Slovenia (Table C27)
1450-1458   Yugoslavia (Table C27)
1495.A-Z   Biography of individual Europeans (not identified with
special subject or country), A-Z
Asia
1498   General works
South Asia
1499   General works

National biography
By region or country
Asia
South Asia -- Continued
Afghanistan see CT1870+

1500-1508	India (Table C27)
1510-1518	Pakistan (Table C27)
1519-1519.8	Bangladesh (Table C28)
1520-1528	Sri Lanka (Table C27)
	Nepal
1529	Collective
1529.2.A-Z	Individual, A-Z
	Subarrange each by Table C30
1530-1538	Burma. Myanmar (Table C27)
1540-1548	Thailand (Table C27)
	Hong Kong
1550	Collective
1552.A-Z	Individual, A-Z
	Subarrange each by Table C30
1560-1568	Malaysia (Table C27)
1570-1578	Singapore (Table C27)
1590-1598	Indonesia (Table C27)
	French Indochina
1630-1638	Vietnam (Table C27)
	Including South Vietnam
1639-1639.8	North Vietnam (Table C28)
1640-1648	Cambodia (Table C27)
1660-1668	Laos (Table C27)
1770-1778	Siberia. Former Soviet Union in Asia (Table C27)
	Central Asia
1779	General works
1779.5.A-Z	Individual countries, A-Z
1779.5.K3-.K38	Kazakhstan (Table C29)
1779.5.K95-.K958	Kyrgyzstan (Table C29)
1790-1798	Philippines (Table C27)
	East Asia
1819	General works
1820-1828	China (Table C27)
	For Hong Kong see CT1550+
1829-1829.8	Taiwan (Table C28)
1830-1838	Japan (Table C27)
1840-1848	Korea (South) (Table C27)
1850-1858	Korea (North) (Table C27)
1859-1859.8	Mongolia (Table C28)
1860-1866	Southwest Asia. Near East. Arab countries (Collectively) (Table C27a)
1870-1878	Afghanistan (Table C27)

	National biography
	By region or country
	Asia
	Southwest Asia. Near East. Arab countries (Collectively)
	-- Continued
1880-1888	Iran (Table C27)
1890-1898	Saudi Arabia (Table C27)
1900-1908	Turkey (Table C27)
1910-1918	Syria (Table C27)
1919.A-Z	Other, A-Z
	Subarrange each by Table C29
1919.A75-.A758	Armenia (Table C29)
1919.A94-.A948	Azerbaijan (Table C29)
1919.C93-.C938	Cyprus (Table C29)
1919.G46-.G468	Georgia (Republic) (Table C29)
1919.L4-.L48	Lebanon (Table C29)
1919.P3-.P38	Palestine. Israel (Table C29)
	Africa
1920	General works
1921-1929	South Africa (Table C27)
1930-1938	Lesotho (Table C27)
1940-1948	Swaziland (Table C27)
1970-1978	Zimbabwe (Table C27)
1980-1988	Botswana (Table C27)
1990-1998	Malawi (Table C27)
2000-2008	Zambia (Table C27)
2010-2018	Namibia (Table C27)
2110-2116	East Africa (Table C27a)
2150-2158	Ethiopia (Table C27)
2200-2208	Somalia (Table C27)
2210-2218	Uganda (Table C27)
2220-2228	Kenya (Table C27)
2230-2238	Tanzania (Table C27)
2240-2248	Mozambique (Table C27)
2250-2258	Rwanda (Table C27)
2270-2278	Madagascar (Table C27)
2280-2288	Mauritius (Table C27)
2290-2298	Réunion (Table C27)
2300-2308	Seychelles (Table C27)
2410-2416	West Africa (Table C27a)
2418-2418.8	Senegal (Table C28)
2419-2419.8	Gambia (Table C28)
2420-2428	Benin (Table C27)
2430-2438	Liberia (Table C27)
2440-2448	Sierra Leone (Table C27)
2460-2468	Côte d'Ivoire. Ivory Coast (Table C27)
2470-2478	Burkina Faso (Table C27)

CT

	National biography
	By region or country
	Africa
	West Africa -- Continued
2500-2508	Ghana (Table C27)
2520-2528	Nigeria (Table C27)
2550-2558	Cameroon (Table C27)
2560-2568	Chad (Table C27)
2580-2588	Zaire (Table C27)
2610-2616	North Africa (Table C27a)
2620-2628	Algeria (Table C27)
2670-2678	Morocco (Table C27)
2690-2698	Tunisia (Table C27)
2700-2708	Libya (Table C27)
2710-2718	Egypt (Table C27)
2730-2738	Sudan (Table C27)
2750.A-Z	Biography of individual Africans (not identified with special subject or country), A-Z
	Oceania. Pacific islands
2775	General works
2800-2808	Australia (Table C27)
2880-2888	New Zealand (Table C27)
2900	Guam
2920	Samoan Islands
2940	Fiji
2950	Papua. New Guinea
2960	Tonga Islands
2980	New Caledonia
2990	Tahiti
3010	Bismark Archipelago
3020	Carolina Islands
3040	Mariana Islands
3050	Marshall Islands
3070	Pelew Islands
3090	Solomon Islands
3150.A-Z	Individuals not identified with any country, A-Z
	Biography. By subject
	Subject biography in the LC Classification System is classed with the pertinent subject field, classes A - Z. The purpose of this section is to provide for special classes of persons not representative of any special subject
	Biography of women (Collective)
	For individual women not associated with a subject field, see CT275 CT310, etc.
3200	Periodicals. Societies. Serials
	General works
3201	Through 1800

Biography. By subject
   Biography of women (Collective)
     General works -- Continued

3202	1801-
3203	General special
	Including women travelers, celebrated beauties, mothers of
	famous persons, etc.
3205	Girls
	Including famous girls
3207	Juvenile works
3210	Ancient
3220	Medieval
	Modern
3230	General works
3232	15th-16th centuries
3233	17th-18th centuries
3234	19th-20th centuries
3235	20th century
	America
3250	General works
	United States
3260	General works
3262.A-Z	By region or state, A-Z
3270	Canada
3285	West Indies
	Latin America
3290	General works
3294	Dominican Republic
3295	Mexico
3297	Costa Rica
3298	Honduras
	South America
3301.5	General works
3302	Argentina
3303	Brazil
3303.5	Chile
3306	Peru
	Europe
3310	General works
	Great Britain. England
3320	General works
3330	Northern Ireland
3340	Scotland
3350	Wales
3410	Austria
3420	France

CT

	Biography. By subject
	Biography of women (Collective)
	Europe -- Continued
3430	Germany
	Including West Germany
3435	East Germany
3440	Greece
3450	Italy
	Low Countries
3470	Netherlands
3480	Belgium
3490	Russia. Former Soviet republics
	Scandinavia
3500	General works
3510	Denmark
3520	Iceland
3530	Norway
3540	Sweden
3560	Spain
3570	Portugal
3600	Balkan States
3650.A-Z	Other European, A-Z
	Asia
3700	General works
3704	Azerbaijan
3705	Burma. Myanmar
3710	China
3715	Taiwan
3720	India
3722	Indonesia
3725	Israel
3730	Japan
3735	Korea
	Including South Korea
3736	North Korea
3737	Lebanon
3738	Malaysia
3739	Nepal
3740	Philippines
3740.5	Saudi Arabia
3741	Thailand
3742	Turkey
3745	Vietnam
	Including South Vietnam
3746	North Vietnam
3748	Arab countries
	Africa

Biography. By subject
 Biography of women (Collective)
  Africa -- Continued

3750	General works
3755	Cameroon
3760	Mali
3770	South Africa
3780	Zimbabwe
3800	Australia
3805	New Zealand
3830	Pacific Islands

Academicians. Scholars. Savants
  Class here scholars eminent in more than one special subject
   area
  For educators, see LA2301+ LB51+ etc.

3990.A2	Collective
3990.A3-Z	Individual, A-Z

Special subjects
  The second edition of Class C provided here by means of
   parenthesized numbers, an alternative treatment of subject
   biography, namely, an arrangement by subject in one
   location. Because these numbers were no longer in
   general use, they were dropped from this edition. An
   individual library still wishing to class subject biography in
   class CT using the earlier scheme should consult the
   second edition
Other miscellaneous groups

9960	Two or more groups

Adventurers

9970	Collective
9971.A-Z	Individual, A-Z

Charlatans, imposters, rogues, scoundrels, etc.
  Cf. HV6751+ Social pathology

9980	Collective
9981.A-Z	Individual, A-Z

People with physical disabilities see HV3012+
Dandies

9985	Collective
9986.A-Z	Individual, A-Z

Eccentrics and curious characters

9990	Collective
9991.A-Z	Individual, A-Z
9992	Midgets. Dwarfs

Men impersonating women

9993.A1	Collective
9993.A2-Z	Individual, A-Z

Women impersonating men

	Biography. By subject
	Other miscellaneous groups
	Women impersonating men -- Continued
9994.A1	Collective
9994.A2-Z	Individual, A-Z
	Misers
9995	Collective
9996.A-Z	Individual, A-Z
	Strong persons
	Class here works dealing with persons of great physical strength not associated with a particular activity or sport
9997.A1	Collective
9997.A2-Z	Individual, A-Z
9998.A-Z	Twins, triplets, quadruplets, etc. By surname, A-Z
9998.D5	Dionne quintuplets
9999	Blank books for personal records, diaries, etc.

	Add the appropriate number from this table to the first number of the classification number span to which the table applies
0	Periodicals. Societies. Serials. Directories
1	General works. History and statistics
2	Inventories (General)
2.A2	Bibliography or lists of inventories
	Subarrange by author, A-Z
	National archives
	Including national and other government archives combined
	At the capital city (or the central archives)
3	History and description
4	Nonofficial
	Including miscellaneous pamphlets
5	Regulations
	For general discussions on organization see C1 3
6	Inventories (General). By date
7.A-Z	Special collections, A-Z
	Subarrange by date
8.A-Z	Special class. By region or country, A-Z
	Special class. By subject
	see bibliography of subject in classes K, M, or Z
9.A-Z	In places other than the capital, A-Z
	Other national government records
11	Agriculture (Table C4)
11.5	Art and antiquities (Table C4)
12	Broadcasting (Table C4)
14	Colonies (Table C4)
15	Commerce (Table C4)
16	Defense (Table C4)
17	Education (Table C4)
17.3	Emigration and immigration (Table C4)
17.5	Foreign affairs (Table C4)
17.6	Forestry (Table C4)
17.7	Health (Table C4)
17.78	Human services (Table C4)
	Immigration see C1 17.3
18	Indian affairs (Table C4)
18.5	Interior (Table C4)
19	Justice (Table C4)
20	Labor (Table C4)
20.2	Post Office (Table C4)
20.5	Privy Council (Table C4)
20.7	Public works (Table C4)
21	Statistics (Table C4)
21.5	Transportation (Table C4)
22	Treasury (Table C4)

TABLES

	National archives -- Continued
23	Heads of state. Presidents. Prime ministers
	For the collected papers of individual heads of state, see classes D-F
	For indexes to the manuscript papers of individual heads of state, see Z6616
	For official documents of a head of a state, see class J
23.5	Parliament. Legislative Branch
	Other local archives
24	General local (divisions treated collectively)
25.A-Z	Provincial, A-Z
	Local (municipal, communal, etc.) treated collectively
26.A1	General works
26.A2	General special. Probate, etc.
26.A4-Z	By province (or other division), A-Z
	Subarrange by author
27.A-Z	Municipal, A-Z
	Including notarial archives
	Parish registers
28.A1	Collective
28.A2A-.A2Z	By diocese, parish, or other division, A-Z
29.A-Z	Religious and academic institutions. By place, A-Z
	Other institutions
	see bibliography of subject in classes K, M, or Z
	Family archives
29.5.A1	Collective
29.5.A3-Z	Individual families, A-Z
	Subarrange each by author

	Add the appropriate number from this table to the first number of the classification number span to which the table applies
0	Periodicals. Societies. Serials. Directories
1	General works. History and statistics
2	Inventories (General)
2.A2	Bibliography or lists of inventories
	Subarrange by author, A-Z
	National archives
	Including national and other government archives combined
	At the capital city (or the central archives)
3	History and description
4	Nonofficial
	Including miscellaneous pamphlets
5	Regulations
	For general discussions on organization see C1a 3
6	Inventories (General). By date
7.A-Z	Special collections, A-Z
	Subarrange by date
8.A-Z	Special class. By region or country, A-Z
	Special class. By subject
	see bibliography of subject in classes K, M, or Z
9.A-Z	In places other than the capital, A-Z
	Other national government records
11	Agriculture (Table C4)
11.5	Art and antiquities (Table C4)
12	Broadcasting (Table C4)
14	Colonies (Table C4)
15	Commerce (Table C4)
16	Defense (Table C4)
17	Education (Table C4)
17.3	Emigration and immigration (Table C4)
17.5	Foreign affairs (Table C4)
17.6	Forestry (Table C4)
17.7	Health (Table C4)
17.78	Human services (Table C4)
	Immigration see C1a 17.3
18	Indian affairs (Table C4)
18.5	Interior (Table C4)
19	Justice (Table C4)
20	Labor (Table C4)
20.2	Post Office (Table C4)
20.5	Privy Council (Table C4)
20.7	Public works (Table C4)
21	Statistics (Table C4)
21.5	Transportation (Table C4)
22	Treasury (Table C4)

TABLES

National archives -- Continued
23   Heads of state. Presidents. Prime ministers
                        For the collected papers of individual heads of state, see classes
                            D-F
                        For indexes to the manuscript papers of individual heads of state,
                            see Z6616
                        For official documents of a head of a state, see class J
23.5   Parliament. Legislative Branch
                 Other local archives
24   General local (divisions treated collectively)

	Add the appropriate number from this table to the first number of the classification number span to which the table applies
0	Periodicals. Societies. Serials. Directories
1	General works. History and statistics
2	Inventories (General)
2.A2	Bibliography or lists of inventories
	Subarrange by author, A-Z
	National archives
	Including national and other government archives combined
	At the capital city (or the central archives)
3	History and description
4	Nonofficial
	Including miscellaneous pamphlets, etc.
5	Regulations
	For general discussions on organization see C2 3
6	Inventories (General). By date
7.A-.Z6	Special collections, A-Z
	Subarrange by date
8.A-Z	Special class. By region or country, A-Z
	Special class. By subject
	see bibliography of subject in classes K, M, or Z
9.A-Z	In places other than the capital, A-Z
	Other national government records
10.5	Agriculture (Table C4)
10.6	Art and antiquities (Table C4)
10.7	Broadcasting (Table C4)
11	Colonies (Table C4)
11.5	Commerce (Table C4)
12	Defense (Table C4)
12.5	Education (Table C4)
12.6	Emigration and immigration (Table C4)
12.7	Foreign affairs (Table C4)
12.8	Forestry (Table C4)
12.9	Health (Table C4)
12.98	Human services (Table C4)
	Immigration see C2 12.6
13	Indian affairs (Table C4)
13.3	Interior (Table C4)
13.5	Justice (Table C4)
14	Labor (Table C4)
14.2	Post Office (Table C4)
14.5	Privy Council (Table C4)
14.7	Public works (Table C4)
14.8	Statistics (Table C4)
14.85	Transportation (Table C4)
15	Treasury (Table C4)

TABLES

	National archives -- Continued
15.25	Heads of state. Presidents. Prime ministers
	For the collected papers of individual heads of state, see classes D-F
	For indexes to the manuscript papers of individual heads of state, see Z6616
	For official documents of a head of a state, see class J
15.5	Parliament. Legislative Branch
	Other local archives
16	General local (divisions treated collectively)
17.A-Z	Provincial, A-Z
	Local (municipal, communal, etc.) treated collectively
17.5.A1	General works
17.5.A2	General special. Probate, etc.
17.5.A4-Z	By province (or other division), A-Z
	Subarrange by author
18.A-Z	Municipal, A-Z
	Including notarial archives
	Parish registers
18.5.A1	Collective
18.5.A2A-.A2Z	By diocese, parish, or other division, A-Z
19.A-Z	Religious and academic institutions. By place, A-Z
	Other institutions
	see bibliography of subject in classes K, M, or Z
	Family archives
19.5.A1	Collective
19.5.A3-Z	Individual families, A-Z
	Subarrange each by author

	Add the appropriate number from this table to the first number of the classification number span to which the table applies
0	Periodicals. Societies. Serials. Directories
1	General works. History and statistics
2	Inventories (General)
2.A2	Bibliography or lists of inventories
	Subarrange by author, A-Z
	National archives
	Including national and other government archives combined
	At the capital city (or the central archives)
3	History and description
4	Nonofficial
	Including miscellaneous pamphlets, etc.
5	Regulations
	For general discussions on organization see C2a 3
6	Inventories (General). By date
7.A-.Z6	Special collections, A-Z
	Subarrange by date
8.A-Z	Special class. By region or country, A-Z
	Special class. By subject
	see bibliography of subject in classes K, M, or Z
9.A-Z	In places other than the capital, A-Z
	Other national government records
10.5	Agriculture (Table C4)
10.6	Art and antiquities (Table C4)
10.7	Broadcasting (Table C4)
11	Colonies (Table C4)
12	Defense (Table C4)
12.5	Education (Table C4)
12.6	Emigration and immigration (Table C4)
12.7	Foreign affairs (Table C4)
12.8	Forestry (Table C4)
12.9	Health (Table C4)
12.98	Human services (Table C4)
	Immigration see C2a 12.6
13	Indian affairs (Table C4)
13.3	Interior (Table C4)
13.5	Justice (Table C4)
14	Labor (Table C4)
14.2	Post Office (Table C4)
14.5	Privy Council (Table C4)
14.7	Public works (Table C4)
14.8	Statistics (Table C4)
14.85	Transportation (Table C4)
15	Treasury (Table C4)

TABLES

National archives -- Continued

15.25   Heads of state. Presidents. Prime ministers
                    For the collected papers of individual heads of state, see classes
                        D-F
                    For indexes to the manuscript papers of individual heads of state,
                        see Z6616
                    For official documents of a head of a state, see class J
15.5   Parliament. Legislative Branch
            Other local archives
16   General local (divisions treated collectively)

Add the appropriate number from this table to the first number of the classification number span to which the table applies

0	Periodicals. Societies. Serials. Directories
1	General works. History and statistics
2	Inventories (General)
2.A2	Bibliography or lists of inventories
	Subarrange by author, A-Z
	National archives
	Including national and other government archives combined
	At the capital city (or the central archives)
3	History and description
4	Inventories (General). By date
4.5.A-Z	Special class. By region or country, A-Z
	Special class. By subject
	see bibliography of subject in classes K, M, or Z
5.A-Z	In places other than the capital, A-Z
	Other national government records
6.15	Agriculture (Table C4)
6.155	Art and antiquities (Table C4)
6.16	Broadcasting (Table C4)
6.18	Colonies (Table C4)
6.23	Commerce (Table C4)
6.26	Defense (Table C4)
6.28	Education (Table C4)
6.3	Emigration and immigration (Table C4)
6.33	Foreign affairs (Table C4)
6.34	Forestry (Table C4)
6.35	Health (Table C4)
6.358	Human services (Table C4)
	Immigration see C3 6.3
6.36	Indian affairs (Table C4)
6.38	Interior (Table C4)
6.43	Justice (Table C4)
6.44	Labor (Table C4)
6.45	Post Office (Table C4)
6.46	Privy Council (Table C4)
6.47	Public works (Table C4)
6.48	Statistics (Table C4)
6.485	Transportation (Table C4)
6.49	Treasury (Table C4)
6.495	Heads of state. Presidents. Prime ministers
	For the collected papers of individual heads of state, see classes D-F
	For indexes to the manuscript papers of individual heads of state, see Z6616
	For official documents of a head of a state, see class J
6.5	Parliament. Legislative Branch

TABLES

	Other local archives
6.9	General local (divisions treated collectively)
7.A-Z	Provincial, A-Z
	Local (municipal, communal, etc.) treated collectively
7.5.A1	General works
7.5.A2	General special. Probate, etc.
7.5.A4-Z	By province (or other division), A-Z
	Subarrange by author
8.A-Z	Municipal, A-Z
	Including notarial archives
	Parish registers
8.5.A1	Collective
8.5.A2A-.A2Z	By diocese, parish, or other division, A-Z
9.A-Z	Religious and academic institutions. By place, A-Z
	Other institutions
	see bibliography of subject in classes K, M, or Z
	Family archives
9.5.A1	Collective
9.5.A3-Z	Individual families, A-Z
	Subarrange each by author

0	General calendars. By date
0.A1-.A4	Serials
0.A5-.A7	Monographs about the archive
0.A8-Z	Bureaus, divisions, agencies within the ministry, etc., A-Z

          Under each:

x	*General calendars. By date*
xA1-A4	*Serials*
xA5-xZ	*Monographs about the bureau, etc.*

TABLES

	Add the appropriate number from this table to the first number of the classification number span to which the table applies
0	Periodicals. Societies. Serials. Directories
	Museums. Collections. Exhibitions
	Public
1	General works
1.2.A-Z	By city, A-Z
	Private
1.3	General works
1.4.A-Z	By collector, A-Z
2	General works
3	General special
	Biography
3.4	Collective
	For collections of the seals and designs of several artists, see the general works number
3.5.A-Z	Individual, A-Z

Under each:

.xA2	Autobiography. By date
.xA4	Reproductions (Collections). By date
.xA8-.xZ	Biography and criticism

    Including collections of the seals and designs of individual artists

	By period
5	Medieval and Renaissance
6	Modern to 1800
7	19th-20th centuries
	Special
9	National, royal, etc.
10	Companies, guilds
11	Ecclesiastic, monastic, etc.
12	Knighthood, orders, etc.
13	Universities, colleges, schools (General)
	For individual institutions, see classes LD-LG
14	Other institutional
15.A-Z	Persons and families, other than royal, A-Z
	Local
17.A-Z	States, provinces, etc., A-Z
18.A-Z	Cities and towns, A-Z

1	Periodicals. Societies. Serials. Directories
	Museums. Collections. Exhibitions
	Public
2	General works
2.2.A-Z	By city, A-Z
	Private
2.3	General works
2.4.A-Z	By collector, A-Z
3	General works
4	General special
	Biography
4.4	Collective
	For collections of the seals and designs of several artists, see the general works number
4.5.A-Z	Individual, A-Z
	Under each:

.xA2	*Autobiography. By date*
.xA4	*Reproductions (Collections). By date*
.xA8-.xZ	*Biography and criticism*

	Including collections of the seals and designs of individual artists
	By period
5	Medieval and Renaissance
6	Modern to 1800
7	19th and 20th centuries
8	Special
9.A-Z	Persons and families, other than royal, A-Z
10.A-Z	Local, A-Z

TABLES

.1	Periodicals. Societies. Serials
	Museums. Collections. Exhibitions
	Public
.2	General works
.22.A-Z	By city, A-Z
	Private
.23	General works
.24.A-Z	By collector, A-Z
.3	General works
.4	General special
	Biography
.44	Collective
	For collections of the seals and designs of several artists, see the general works number
.45.A-Z	Individual, A-Z

    Under each:

.xA2	*Autobiography. By date*
.xA4	*Reproductions (Collections). By date*
.xA8-.xZ	*Biography and criticism*

    Including collections of the seals and designs of individual artists

	By period
.5	Medieval and Renaissance
.6	Modern to 1800
.7	19th-20th centuries
.8	Special
.9.A-Z	Persons and families, other than royal, A-Z
.95.A-Z	Local, A-Z

	Add the appropriate number from this table to the first number of the classification number span to which the table applies
0	Periodicals. Societies. Serials
(1)	Yearbooks
	see C8 0
2	Collected works (nonserial)
	Museums. Collections. Exhibitions
	Public
4	General works
4.2.A-Z	By city, A-Z
	Private
5	General works
5.2.A-Z	By collector, A-Z
6	Sales catalogs. Coin values
9	Dictionaries. Directories
10	General works
12	General special
	Coins of special materials
14	Gold
15	Silver
16	Bronze and copper
17	Other (not A-Z)
19	Iconography
	Biography of coin designers
20	Collective
20.5.A-Z	Individual, A-Z
	By period
21	Medieval
22	Early modern to 1789/1815
24	Early 19th century, 1789/1815 through 1870
25	Later 19th and 20th centuries, 1871-
	Local
28.A-Z	States, provinces, etc., A-Z
29.A-Z	Cities and towns, A-Z

TABLES

	Add the appropriate number from this table to the first number of the classification number span to which the table applies
0	Periodicals. Societies. Serials
	Museums. Collections. Exhibitions
	Public
2	General works
2.2.A-Z	By city, A-Z
	Private
3	General works
3.2.A-Z	By collector, A-Z
4	Sales catalogs. Coin values
5	Dictionaries. Directories
6	General works
7	General special
	Coins of special materials
8	Gold
9	Silver
10	Bronze and copper
11	Other (not A-Z)
12	Iconography
	Biography of coin designers
13	Collective
13.5.A-Z	Individual, A-Z
	By period
14	Medieval
15	Early modern to 1789/1815
16	Early 19th century, 1789/1815 through 1870
17	Later 19th and centuries, 1971-
19.A-Z	Local, A-Z

Add the appropriate number from this table to the first number of the classification number span to which the table applies

0	Periodicals. Societies. Serials
	Museums. Collections. Exhibitions
	Public
2	General works
2.2.A-Z	By city, A-Z
	Private
3	General works
3.2.A-Z	By collector, A-Z
4	Sales catalogs. Coin values
5	Dictionaries. Directories
6	General works
7	General special
9.A-Z	Local, A-Z

TABLES

1	Periodicals. Societies. Serials
2	Catalogs
3	General works
4	General special
	By period
5	Medieval
6	16th-18th centuries
7	19th-20th centuries
	Local, A-Z
9.A-Z	States, provinces, etc.
10.A-Z	Cities, towns, etc.

1	Periodicals. Societies. Serials
2	Catalogs
3	General works
4	General special
5.A-Z	Local, A-Z

TABLES

1	Periodicals. Societies. Serials
2	Catalogs
3	General works
4	General special

1	Periodicals. Societies. Serials
	Museums
	Public
2	General works
2.2.A-Z	By city, A-Z
	Private
3	General works
3.3.A-Z	By collector, A-Z
4	Sales catalogs
5	General works
6	General special
	For works on medals relating to a special subject, see CJ5793
	Biography of medalists
8	Collective
9.A-Z	Individual artists, A-Z
	By period
10	Medieval
11	Renaissance, 15th-17th centuries
12	18th century
13	19th-20th centuries
15.A-Z	Persons and families, A-Z
	Class here medals of individuals and families in all fields
17.A-Z	Events, A-Z
	Local, A-Z
18.A-Z	States, provinces, etc.
19.A-Z	Cities, towns, etc.

TABLES

1	Periodicals. Societies. Serials
1.5	Sales catalogs
2	General works
3	General special
	For works on medals relating to a special subject, see CJ5793
	Biography of medalists
3.3	Collective
3.5.A-Z	Individual artists, A-Z
	By period
4	Medieval
5	18th century
6	19th-20th centuries
7.A-Z	Persons and families, A-Z
	Class here medals of individuals and families in all fields
8.A-Z	Events, A-Z
9.A-Z	Local, A-Z

1	Periodicals. Societies. Serials
1.5	Sales catalogs
2	General works
3	General special
	For works on medals relating to a special subject, see CJ5793
	Biography of medalists
3.3	Collective
3.5.A-Z	Individual artists, A-Z
	By period
4	Medieval
5	18th century
6	19th-20th centuries
7.A-Z	Persons and families, A-Z
	Class here medals of individuals and families in all fields
8.A-Z	Events, A-Z

1	Periodicals. Societies. Serials
1.5	Sales catalogs
2	General works
3	General special
	For works on medals relating to a special subject, see CJ5793
	Biography of medalists
3.3	Collective
3.5.A-Z	Individual, A-Z
4.A-Z	Persons and families, A-Z
	Class here medals of individuals and families in all fields
5.A-Z	Local, A-Z

	Add the appropriate number from this table to the first number of the classification number span to which the table applies
0	Periodicals. Societies. Serials
	Heralds (Kings-at-arms)
	see CR183+
2	National
	Including general albums, etc.
	Cf. CD, Seals
	States, provinces, counties, etc.
3.A1-.A5	General works
3.A6-Z	By state, etc., A-Z
	Cities and towns
4.A1-.A5	General works
	By province (or other subdivision) see C16 3.A1+
4.A6-Z	By individual city, A-Z
	Special
	Guilds
5.A1-.A5	General works
5.A6-Z	By trade, A-Z
6.A-Z	City companies. By city, A-Z
	Under each:

.x	*General works*
.x2A-.x2Z	*Special. By company, A-Z*

7	Universities and colleges
	Class here general works only. For college colors, insignia, etc., see LB3630; individual institutions, see classes LD-LG; student fraternities, see LJ53
8	Schools
	Class here general works only. For school colors, insignia, etc., see LB3630; individual institutions, see classes LD-LG
9	Other institutions

	Add the appropriate number from this table to the first number of the classification number span to which the table applies
0	Periodicals. Societies. Serials
	Heralds (Kings-at-arms)
	see CR183+
1	National
	Including general albums, etc.
	Cf. CD, Seals
	States, provinces, counties, etc.
2.A1-.A5	General works
2.A6-Z	By state, etc., A-Z
	Cities and towns
3.A1-.A5	General works
	By province (or other subdivision) see C17 2.A1+
3.A6-Z	By individual city, A-Z
4	Special

Add the appropriate number from this table to the first number of the classification number span to which the table applies

0	Periodicals. Societies. Serials
1	Collected works (nonserial)
2	General works
3	General special
	By period
4	Early and medieval
5	16th-18th centuries
6	19th-20th centuries
8	Dictionaries. Encyclopedias
9	General albums, lists of armorial families, etc.
	By class
10	Royal arms (Sovereign houses)
	Nobility
11	Nobility in general
12	Higher ranks
13	Lower ranks
14	Armorial families other than noble
15.A-Z	Other classes, A-Z
	By place
17.A-Z	States, provinces, counties, etc., A-Z
18.A-Z	Cities and towns, A-Z
19.A-Z	Families, individuals, and lordships, A-Z

TABLES

Add the appropriate number from this table to the first number of the
classification number span to which the table applies

0	Periodicals. Societies. Serials
1	General works
	By period
2	Early and medieval
3	19th-20th centuries
4	General albums, lists of armorial families, etc.
5	By class (Royal arms, nobility, armorial families)
	By place
7.A-Z	States, provinces, counties, etc., A-Z
8.A-Z	Cities and towns, A-Z
9.A-Z	Families, individuals, and lordships, A-Z

	Add the appropriate number from this table to the first number of the classification number span to which the table applies
0	Periodicals. Societies. Serials
1	General works
	By period
2	Early and medieval
3	19th-20th centuries
4	General albums, lists of armorial families, etc.
5	By class (Royal arms, nobility, armorial families)
9.A-Z	Families, individuals, and lordships, A-Z

TABLES

	Add the appropriate number from this table to the first number of the classification number span to which the table applies
0	Periodicals. Societies. Serials
1	General works
	History
2	General works
3	Early
4	Medieval
5	Modern
	Special topics
6	Usurpation of titles, etc.
7	Particle of nobility
8	Order of precedence
9	Other special (not A-Z)
	Including law of peerage

Add the appropriate number from this table to the first number of the classification number span to which the table applies

0	Periodicals. Societies. Serials
1	General works
2	History
3	Special topics

	Add the appropriate number from this table to the first number of the classification number span to which the table applies
0	Periodicals. Societies. Serials
1	Directories
2	Dictionaries. Encyclopedias
3	General works
4	General special
	By class
6	Royalty and the court
	Aristocracy and nobility
7	General works
8	Peerage
9	Other nobility
10	Gentry
11	Commoners
	By period
12	Early
13	Medieval
14	Modern
16.A-Z	Special topics, A-Z
16.A25	Acadians
16.A52	Amish
16.A57	Apprentices
16.B62	Boatmen
16.B74	Brethren (Brethren churches)
16.C37	Catholics
16.C44	Celebrities
16.C56	Church records and registers
16.C6	Coal miners
16.C66	Court records
16.H83	Huguenots
16.J33	Jacobites
16.J4	Jews
16.K37	Karelians
16.L87	Lutherans
16.M3	Marshalls
16.M46	Mennonites
16.M54	Millionaires
16.M67	Mormons
16.P3	Palatines
16.P64	Popes
16.P66	Presbyterians
16.P67	Presidents
16.P7	Priests
16.P75	Protestants
16.Q35	Quakers
16.S34	Salzburgers

	Special topics, A-Z -- Continued
16.S36	Scots
16.S68	Society of the Cincinnati
16.S69	Soldiers
	Local (Not elsewhere provided for)
	Including wills, sepulchral records, registers of marriages, births, deaths, etc.
	For contested will cases, see class K
17.A1	Collective
17.A3-Z	By province (or other division), A-Z
	Family history
18	Collective (other than local)
19.A-Z	Individual, A-Z
	Under each, assign 2 successive Cutter numbers as follows:
	(1) Periodicals. Serials
	(2) General works. By date

TABLES

	Add the appropriate number from this table to the first number of the classification number span to which the table applies
0	Periodicals. Societies. Serials
1	Directories
2	General works
3	General special
	By class
4	Royalty and nobility in general
5	Commoners
	By period
6	Early
7	Modern
	Special topics see C23 3
	Local (Not elsewhere provided for)
	Including wills, sepulchral records, registers of marriages, births, deaths, etc.
	For contested will cases, see class K
8.A1	Collective
8.A3-Z	By province (or other subdivision), A-Z
	Family history
9.A2	Collective
9.A3-Z	Individual, A-Z
	Under each:
	.x *Periodicals. Serials*
	.x2 *General works. By date*

.A1-.Z7	General works
.Z8A-.Z8Z	Particular names, A-Z
.Z9A-.Z9Z	Local, A-Z

TABLES

	Add the appropriate number from this table to the first number of the classification number span to which the table applies
0	Collections
1	General works
3	Early and medieval
	Forenames
	see CS2367+
5	Surnames. Family names
7	General special
8.A-Z	Particular names, A-Z
9.A-Z	Local, A-Z

	Add the appropriate number from this table to the first number of the classification number span to which the table applies
0	Periodicals. Societies. Serials
1	Collected works (nonserial)
2	Early works through 1800
3	Dictionaries. Encyclopedias
4	General works, 1801-
5	General special
7	Juvenile works
7.5	Portraits
	By period
	Ancient
	see class D
	Medieval
	see class D
	Modern
10	15th-16th centuries
11	17th-18th centuries
12	19th-20th centuries
13	20th century
13.5	21st century
(14)	Colonies
	see CT280+
(15.A-Z)	Local divisions, A-Z
	Class here collective biographies of persons not classed in classes D - F; for individual biography, see 18
	Cities
	see class D
	Rulers
	see classes D - F
17.A-Z	Individual families, A-Z
	Individual persons
	For individual biographies of political or historical persons, or of persons associated with particular cities, see classes D-F
18.A-.Z8	By name, A-Z
	Subarrange each by Table C30
18.Z9	Persons not known by name

TABLES

	Add the appropriate number from this table to the first number of the classification number span to which the table applies
0	Periodicals. Societies. Serials
1	Collected works (nonserial)
2	Dictionaries. Encyclopedias
3	General works
4	General special
4.3	Juvenile works
4.5	Portraits
	By period
	Ancient
	see class D
	Medieval
	see class D
	Modern
5	Through 1800
6	1801-
7.A-Z	Local divisions, A-Z
	Class here collective biographies of persons not classed in classes D-F; for individual biography, see C27 8
	Cities
	see classes D-F
	Rulers
	see classes D-F
7.5.A-Z	Individual families, A-Z
8.A-Z	Individual persons, A-Z
	For individual biographies of political or historical persons, or of persons associated with particular cities, see classes D - F
8.Z9	Persons not known by name

Add the appropriate number from this table to the first number of the
classification number span to which the table applies

0	Periodicals. Societies. Serials
1	Collected works (nonserial)
2	Dictionaries. Encyclopedias
3	General works
4	General special
4.3	Juvenile works
4.5	Portraits
	By period
	Ancient
	see class D
	Medieval
	see class D
	Modern
5	Through 1800
6	1801-

TABLES

0	Periodicals. Societies. Serials
0.1	Collected works (nonserial)
0.2	Dictionaries. Encyclopedias
0.3	General works
0.4	General special
0.43	Juvenile works
0.45	Portraits
	By period
	Ancient
	see class D
	Medieval
	see class D
	Modern
0.5	Through 1800
0.6	1801-
0.7.A-Z	Local divisions, A-Z
	Class here collective biographies of persons not classed in classes D-F; for individual biography, see .8
	Cities
	see classes D-F
	Rulers
	see classes D-F
0.75.A-Z	Individual families, A-Z
0.8.A-Z	Individual persons, A-Z
	For individual biographies of political or historical persons, or of persons associated with particular cities, see classes D-F
0.8.Z9	Persons not known by name

.x	Periodicals. Societies. Serials
.x2	Collected works (nonserial)
.x3	General works
.x4	General special
.x43	Juvenile works
.x45	Portraits
	By period
	Ancient
	see class D
	Medieval
	see class D
.x5	Modern
.x7A-.x7Z	Local divisions, A-Z
	For political or historical persons, see classes D-F
	Cities
	see classes D-F
	Rulers
	see classes D-F
.x75A-.x75Z	Individual families, A-Z
.x8A-.x8Z	Individual biography, A-Z
.x8Z9-.x8Z99	Persons not known by name

TABLES

.xA2	Collected works. By date
.xA25	Selected works. Selections. By date
	Including quotations
.xA3	Autobiography, diaries, etc. By date
.xA4	Letters. By date
.xA5	Speeches, essays, and lectures. By date
.xA6-.xZ	Biography and criticism

0	Periodicals. Societies. Serials
1	General history and statistics
4	State archives
6.A-Z	State departments, A-Z
	e.g.
6.S8	State Department
6.5	Legislative Branch (Table C4)
	Counties
7.A1	General works
7.A2-Z	By county, A-Z
	Municipal
8.A1	General works
8.A2-Z	By municipality, A-Z
	Parish registers
8.5	Collective
8.6.A-Z	By diocese, parish, or other division, A-Z
9.A-Z	Religious and academic institutions. By place, A-Z
	Other institutions
	see bibliography of subject in classes K, M, or Z
	Family archives
	see CD3029.5

TABLES

INDEX

GPO U.S. GOVERNMENT PRINTING OFFICE: 2008–340–014/60020